DEEPLY
ROOTED

A forty day journey to cultivate
a powerful and life-giving
relationship with God

BY STACEY BEEBE

DEEPLY ROOTED

ISBN: 978-1-7361718-0-6

The Grafting Project
Holland, MI

Cover design by Tami Boyce (www.tamiboyce.com)

DEDICATION

This book is gratefully dedicated to God, my compassionate Father, Jesus my closest Friend, and the Holy Spirit, my undaunted Helper and Encourager.

To the One Who has never left my side
The Healer of my heart and my body
My Playmate as a lonely child
My Security amid trauma and turmoil
My Courage when trembling with fear
My Strength in weakness
My Hope in the waiting
My Joy in the midst of suffering
My Comfort in grief
My Provider in desolation
My Exuberant Guide through life's many adventures and challenges
You are my Everything!

*"My flesh and my heart may fail, but God is the
strength of my heart and my portion forever."*
Psalm 73:26

ACKNOWLEDGMENTS

To my wonderful husband and partner in the Gospel, Brandon, I thank God every day for you and for the way you share God's heart with me. I could not have done any of this without your constant support and encouragement. I am so glad that God teamed us up! Team Beebe for Jesus!

To author, speaker, and mentor, Graham Cooke (brilliantperspectives.com), thank you for being a living example of a powerful life built on a personal intimacy with God. The Kingdom legacy you continue to build truly demonstrates that "one person, walking with God, is always in the majority." You are a "man of a different spirit" who has truly turned the world upside down!

To author, speaker, spiritual General, and friend, Allison Bown (*Joyful Intentionality*, and *The Image*), thank you for showing me how to dig deep for every treasure God has for me. You are a gifted teacher and tool maker that takes powerful and beautiful spiritual principles and helps others (especially me) walk those truths out in our day-to-day lives. You have shown me how to develop a personal, dynamic relationship with God that does not sway with my feelings, and you have shown me how to take every difficulty and make it a spiritual launching point where God transforms me from "one degree of glory to another." (II Cor. 3:18)

To author, speaker, Executive Director of The Warrior Commission, and friend, Christine Casten (*All God Created You to Be: A Journey to Identity*), thank you for your humble leadership, guidance, and encouragement. You have shown me the Kingdom power of pouring yourself out in order to lift others up. You encouraged me to step out of my comfort zone MANY years ago. (Remember the Exploration Round Table?) In so doing, you set me on a path of discovering with God who He created me to be and who He is calling me to become, as His ambassador in this world. You have walked alongside me through many seasons, as God so lovingly molded (and continues to mold) me into His image.

To my spiritual family and band of brothers and sisters, *The Warrior Commission*, including all of those mentioned above, who have built and shaped this amazing community (thewarriorcommission.com), thank you for showing me what true discipleship actually looks like. There is nothing more powerful than a community of passionate lovers of Jesus, linking arms and exploring all that is on God's heart together in unity. I am constantly encouraged and inspired by each one of you, and I love watching you discover and grow into all that God has created you to be. You are all world-changing spiritual giants, and I am humbled and honored to call you my friends.

To my dear and precious church family, Community Church of Douglas (ccofdouglas.org), Brandon and I have been so blessed and honored that God has called us to serve with you. We are so grateful for all of your prayers and support this past year as we have come to call you home. Thank you for your love, generosity, and service to us and to our greater community. I am BEYOND EXCITED for all that God has in store for us together as we grow in His love for us and His passion to care for the lost and the hurting in our area.

ACKNOWLEDGMENTS

To my new friend and editor, Jill Boyce (jpbwrite@yahoo.com), thank you for your tireless and prayer-filled work in transforming my humble and insufficient words into a message that brings God's heart to those who will read this by the power of the Holy Spirit. I have been blessed to be able to create this with you as we listened to God's voice together...WHAT AN INDESCRIBABLE BLESSING!

TABLE OF CONTENTS

INTRODUCTION

CREATED FOR RELATIONSHIP

There is something inherently beautiful about a garden. Gardens call to us. As we walk through a well-tended garden, something in us shifts. Time slows down. Our pace slows. Our breathing becomes deeper and calmer. We pause to admire and enjoy. We notice the scents in the air and the caress of the breeze on our skin. The silky softness of a flower and the rough texture of rugged tree bark both equally delight our sense of touch. The sweet aroma of flowers surround us. We are drawn into an experience, and our souls cry out for deep connection. Our spirits begin to come alive. The voice of God reverberates through all of creation, and we are compelled to come running to Him.

"Nature is too thin a screen; the glory of the omnipresent God bursts through everywhere." (Ralph Waldo Emerson)

It is no wonder, then, that the story of human history both begins and ends in a garden. The books of Genesis and Revelation remind us where we belong. They remind us that we were made to have a powerful and life-giving relationship with our Creator.

EVE'S STORY

I awake in the garden. The sun is rising. Shafts of light are breaking through the trees. The air is cool and gentle. Every day here is beautiful. Every day is perfect. There is a sound riding on the breeze – a sound like softly falling rain – a familiar sound that warms my heart and lifts my head every time I hear it. It's the sound of my Creator calling to me. He is calling my name – the name that He gave me when He formed me. He knows every part of me, and He loves me. As He makes His way down the path, it seems like everything begins to hum with vibrant life. The flowers begin to blossom, and the animals call out with joy. Those shafts of light are now overpowered by His radiant face as He draws closer. His eyes wash over me with indescribable love, and at once, I am made whole. My God. My Creator. My Friend. He reaches out His huge and majestic arms and embraces me with a tenderness beyond understanding. We walk together now – chatting, laughing, crying. He recounts to me once again the story of how He made me, and His voice resounds with so much love and compassion. "They will never be alone," He whispers to Himself, and as He gazes off into the distance, He suddenly takes on a look of deep sadness – desperate longing. His face reflects the grief of a Father Who has lost His Son. A moment of painful stillness deafens the sky. Then, with resolute determination, He turns to me and says, "Don't worry. You will never be alone."

We were created to be in relationship with God. We were never meant to be separated. Through the ages, we have found countless ways to run away from Him and hide, just like Adam and Eve did. We keep ourselves busy, telling ourselves we will get around to God when we have time. If we can't keep hiding from Him, we try to earn our way back into His grace – somehow make ourselves worthy of Him. But we can't. We put on our proper "fig leaves," our Sunday best, our white-washed smiles, and our greetings of, "I'm fine and how are you?" We try to work hard, do what we are supposed to do, and behave in just the right ways. We convince ourselves that if we just try a little harder, then maybe everything will be okay, yet we still feel isolated and alone. It feels like God is somehow beyond our reach, but this is not why we were created. This is not why He sent His son to live, die, and rise again. He did not create us to be His servants. He created us to be His friends.

John 15:15 says, "*I have not called you servants, but friends.*"

No matter how far we run, how distant we feel from Him, or how hard we try to hide our true selves from Him, there is one thing we can be utterly sure of. Nothing can separate us from His love.

> *Roman 8:38-39 "For I am convinced that neither death nor life, neither angels nor demons, neither the present nor the future, nor any powers, neither height, nor depth, nor anything else in all creation, will be able to separate us from the love of God that is in Christ Jesus our Lord."*

He seeks us out. He calls out to us. He reaches out to us with resolute, unshakable determination until we reach back and take His hand. This is the beautiful journey that we are undertaking together – a journey back into relationship – a journey back into a lifestyle of encountering the presence, the touch, the voice, and the heart of God.

 **PRAYER**

Jesus, thank You for your unwavering passion to restore me to a right and real relationship with You. Thank You that it is Your heart's desire that I know You, that I experience You, that I hear Your voice. It's by Your grace, and I choose to respond to your call. Here I am, Lord. Take me on this journey of knowing You more.

Amen.

WEEK ONE

DEEPLY ROOTED IN THE CHARACTER OF GOD

WHEN WE REALIZE GOD IS GREATER THAN WE HOPED HE WOULD BE

WEEK ONE:

DEEPLY ROOTED
IN THE CHARACTER
OF GOD

WHEN WE REALIZE GOD
IS GREATER THAN WE
HOPED HE WOULD BE

> *"The goodness of God is infinitely more wonderful than we will ever be able to comprehend."*
> A.W. Tozer

"Who compares with you among gods, O God?
Who compares with you in power, in holy majesty,
in awesome praises, wonder-working God?"
(Exodus 15:11 The Message)

MONDAY

GOD IS GREATER THAN WE CAN IMAGINE

As Christians, we have the awe-inspiring privilege of spending the rest of eternity exploring and experiencing the vast goodness of God, and what's even more amazing is that this journey begins now! Every time we turn our attention toward God to seek His face, every moment that we stop to rest in His presence, every time our hearts cry out to Him in the midst of our struggles, we receive from Him a greater understanding of Who He is and What He is like. In fact, the Truth of Who He is in our lives is always better than what we hoped for, because He is greater than we can imagine!

The scripture passage above was a song that was sung by Moses after God parted the sea and led the Israelites to freedom from Egypt. What an eye-opening encounter with the saving power of God that must have been! Who dared to dream, before this moment, that God could create a dry path through the sea in an instant? In that moment, they realized that God was greater than they had ever imagined, and they were left praising and worshipping together safely on the shore!

Yet this was not the end of Moses' journey with the character of God. He did not have this one miraculous encounter and then hang up his hat. So often we rest on what God did for us at the moment of salvation, or a past experience we had with Him, but God wants to show us something new about Himself every day. In fact, He so desperately longs for us to know Him more fully, that He just waits for any excuse we give Him to show us how powerful and loving and good He is!

It was not long after this amazing revelation that Moses had another opportunity to be awestruck by how great God is. He had found himself wandering through the desert in charge of this multitude of lost, hungry, and complaining people. He was in a situation far greater than he could handle in his own strength. He was desperate. He had come face-to-face with his own limitations, and he knew that only one thing could bring the breakthrough he needed – an encounter with the living God. He was in a new situation that required a new experience of Who God was. He understood that God was glorious. He remembered what God had done for them. He had held onto God's promises somehow, through many years of wandering. He didn't need to be reminded, but he needed to see God, to feel Him, and to be changed by Him. He needed it so badly, that he was willing to die for it. Meeting God became the only thing that mattered, and God graciously and lovingly responded to Moses' cry.

# WHEN GOD MET WITH MOSES (BASED ON EXODUS 33:12-24:6)

It is oppressively dark and cold here. I feel the dampness of this rock deep in my bones. It was His great hand that set me here, but I need to see Him. I need to know, even if it kills me, which it very well might. I am in so far over my head. I am a murderer and a sheep herder – a nobody. Now I am leading an entire nation through the

desert. *I have no idea what I am doing. The wind is picking up. I am desperate – so desperate! Where are You, God? I need to see Your Glory! I can't do this without You! I need more of You!*

Wait. Is that a shaft of light breaking through? I feel so alone against such a great multitude. The ground is beginning to rumble. Small rocks are breaking free from the walls and hitting the ground like rain. Maybe I will die after all. I've been too presumptuous with a Holy God, but I need Him, and I won't go on without Him. Suddenly, a blinding light engulfs the little cleft. The earth trembles, and the mountains shake. A loud and thunderous voice rends the skies. This is it. This is my death.

"I AM THE LORD YOUR GOD! I AM GRACIOUS AND COMPASSIONATE, SLOW TO ANGER, ABOUNDING IN LOVE AND FAITHFULNESS."

I sit silent and stunned and trembling, as the weight of His Holy words settle in my soul. Instead of judgement, He spoke His Grace. Instead of anger, He filled me with His Compassion. Instead of death, I am consumed by His unspeakable Love. As the full truth of who He is hits me, I am undone. I fall facedown and weep in love and gratitude. I will never be the same.

This encounter with God changed Moses' understanding of what God is like. It was in this moment that Moses became more deeply rooted in the character of God.

 # BECOMING ROOTED

So how do we become rooted in the character of God? Think about a tree that has just been planted. In that moment, the roots of the tree have an encounter with the nutrients in the soil that is life-sustaining. But that is not the end of the story of the tree. It does not remain the same. As the tree discovers that the soil is good and full of nutrients, it begins a never-ending process of stretching its roots deeper and deeper into the soil. As the tree grows, it is no longer satisfied with just a square foot of soil. The roots reach out to encounter more and more of the vast soil and varying nutrients that surround it.

This is how we begin the process of becoming deeply rooted in God's character. As we grow in Him, we are no longer satisfied with just the encounter and understanding of God that we received at the moment of salvation. We get to stretch out our hearts to receive and experience how vast God is, and this journey never ends! The apostle Paul put it this way about the love of God:

> *"And I pray that you, being rooted and established in love, may*
> *have power, together with all the Lord's holy people, to grasp*
> *how wide and long and high and deep is the love of Christ, and*
> *to know this love that surpasses understanding, that you may*
> *be filled to the measure of all the fullness of God."*
> *(Ephesians 3:17-19)*

No matter what your current situation is, or what your past experiences have been, God longs for you to have an encounter with Him. He wants you to know what He is truly like.

What if we were willing to make ourselves vulnerable to Him and truly cry out for an encounter with Him? What if we stepped beyond our fears and our past hurts? What if we put aside our doubts and our limited expectations? What if we asked Him to show us who He really is? If you are willing, would you pray this Moses prayer with me?

 **PRAYER**

God, I need You. I don't just need to know more about You. I need to meet with You, face to face. *God, show me Your glory!* For I know that only by encountering You, will I be changed forever into Your image. Only by hearing Your voice will I find true life, and only by feeling Your love, will I be made whole. Come, Lord. I know that You are drawing me to You and that You will come running to meet me.

Amen.

 REACHING DEEPER

If you are like the vast majority of us, you probably never had God part a sea before you or visibly pass before you and audibly proclaim Who He is. In fact, maybe you can't even think of a time when you had an experience with God's character. Tomorrow we will walk through a tangible, practical exercise that will take you from wherever you are right now to a greater encounter with the character of God. The great news is that it is not up to us. God longs to reveal Himself to us. In fact, He even gave us this firm promise: *"You will seek me and find me when you seek me with all your heart."* (Jer. 29:13)

WEEK ONE:

DEEPLY ROOTED IN THE CHARACTER OF GOD

WHEN WE REALIZE GOD IS GREATER THAN WE HOPED HE WOULD BE

TUESDAY

 ## AN EXERCISE IN GOING DEEPER

Yesterday we learned that God is greater than anything we can imagine, yet it is our indescribable joy to be able to continually explore the heights, the depths, and the breadth of all that God is.

So where do we begin this expansive exploration? We begin by discovering where we are. For example, when looking at a map before going on a journey, the first place we look for is the "You are here" sticker. Understanding where God has brought us to at this point in our lives and recognizing the ways in which God has shown Himself to us in our past, will help orient us as we set out on this amazing discovery of the character of God.

I have provided some questions for you to think about with God. This is not a test. This is a place to start a life-long conversation with God about Who He is and what He is like. Take your time with Him. Find a quiet place where you can sit with Him. If you don't answer every question, that is okay. Let Him guide you. Let Him show you what He wants you to see. No matter the outcome, enjoy spending time with Him. Know that just being with you is what His heart most longs for, and remember His promise:

> *"You will seek me and find me when you*
> *seek me with all your heart."*
> *(Jer. 29:13)*

QUESTIONS/ACTIVITIES

1. In the back of this book, I have created a list of some of the names and characteristics of God. Turn to Appendix #One and take some time to look them over. Slowly read through them, and consider the truth in them. I highly recommend that you read this list out loud. Say, "God, You are..." There is something powerful – and worshipful – in hearing your own voice declaring to God Who He is to you.

2. Look through the list again, and think about a time when God showed Himself to you as one of these Names. Write down the story here and the name that He was for you.

_____

_____

_____

_____

_____

3. Thank God for showing Himself to you in this way.

_____

_____

_____

_____

4. Put that Name or characteristic in the blanks in the prayer below.

5. Keep asking God to show you more about this Name. Ask Him to help you to be able to grasp how wide and long and high and deep this Name is, until you overflow with this characteristic.

"And I pray that you, being rooted and established in love, may have power, together with all the Lord's holy people, to grasp how wide and long and high and deep is the love of Christ, and to know this love that surpasses understanding, that you may be filled to the measure of all the fullness of God."
(Ephesians 3:17-19)

6. The ways in which God has revealed Himself to you points to a gift that He has given you, so that you might pass that gift on to someone else. For example, if you experienced comfort from God, you are now a carrier of His comfort for others. Rewrite that name or characteristic here.

_____

7. Ask God if there is someone in your life that needs to have an encounter with that aspect of God's character. For example, do you know someone who needs to experience God's comfort? Write their name here.

_____

8. Ask God how you can express that characteristic to that person this week. Write down what He shows you.

_____

_____

_____

_____

_____

9. Be intentional this week about following through on what God showed you in Question #7. Write down how it went.

_____

_____

_____

_____

_____

"Praise be to the God and Father of our Lord Jesus Christ, the Father of compassion and the God of all comfort, who comforts us in all our troubles, so that we can comfort those in any trouble with the comfort we ourselves receive from God."
(2 Corinthians 1:3-4)

 # BECOMING DEEPLY ROOTED

Something amazing happens when the roots of a tree begin to dig into the soil around it. The nourishment from the soil makes its way to the branches, where leaves appear and fruit begins to blossom!

In this exercise, you began to discover the ways in which God has shown His character to you. Like the roots of a tree that actively receive nourishment from the soil, you intentionally connected to the ways God has shared His heart with you. Just as the tree draws nourishment from the soil into its branches where leaves appear and fruit blossoms, you are learning how to actively take the encounters you have had with God into your heart and actions, where you can become a blessing to others!

 **PRAYER**

God, thank You for the ways You have shown Yourself to me throughout my life. Thank You for being my _(who God has been for you)_ when I needed You. Remind me of what that felt like, and show me how I can be a carrier of Your _(who God has been for you)_ to those around me.

Amen.

WEEK ONE:

DEEPLY ROOTED IN THE CHARACTER OF GOD

WHEN WE REALIZE GOD IS GREATER THAN WE HOPED HE WOULD BE

"Knowing God is like listening to beautiful music. His words have power. He lifts me up and soothes my soul. He makes me dance. He gives me joy."
(Germany Kent)

"Be still and know that I am God."
(Psalm 46:10)

WEDNESDAY

 ## DO YOU KNOW GOD, OR DO YOU *KNOW* GOD?

Have you ever crammed for a test at the last minute or used mental tricks like a pneumonic in order to remember a list of names or dates? Have you stayed up all night to learn something, only to have 99% of it fall out of your brain just moments after the test?

We spend a large portion of our lives being assessed on what we know. Unfortunately, in western culture, this has often translated to our relationship with God. In Sunday school, we would have Bible drills, scripture memorization quizzes, and even historical lessons. As adults, many of us continue to pursue biblical knowledge. Don't get me wrong, these are not bad things. In fact, they can be very helpful. But gathering information about God, by itself, will never lead to a transformational relationship with God.

In our culture, when someone uses the phrase *to know*, it conjures up an image of the brain – a mental download of facts. In contrast, the phrase *to know* in Hebrew is the word *Yada*. This word is derived from the word *Yad* which means *hand*. In order to *know* something with your hand, you have to touch it, feel it, experience it. Therefore, we cannot truly know something about God without having a tangible encounter with that truth.

There is a significant difference between the heart of someone who knows that God loves them because they read it in the

Bible, and the heart of someone who knows that God loves them because they have felt His loving arms wrap around them as He whispers, "I love you."

 # WHEN I *KNEW*

I grew up in the church. I loved to sing the song "Jesus Loves Me" as a child. In fact, I loved Jesus with all my little heart. However, I never really felt loved or valuable. I grew up with deep wounds. I was extremely withdrawn. I felt insecure and unsafe most of the time.

As I got older and moved away to college, God began to bring people into my life who started to help me feel accepted just as I was. They understood what it was like to experience God's heart, and shared that heart with me. As God continued to draw me closer and closer to Him in this way, I found myself desperately longing to be able to feel God's love for me in a way I hadn't felt it before. One day I was at church, and as worship began, I heard this undeniable voice pierce my heart with the words, "I love you so much." I could feel the passion in God's voice. It reached in, grabbed my heart, and began unraveling all of the pain I had been carrying for so long. It took my breath away and gave me new breath at the same time. I began weeping uncontrollably. I was so undone by the intensity of His heart that I just crumpled to the floor between the seats, and I stayed there for quite some time.

This was my almost daily experience for several months. I would begin to worship and immediately be overcome by His love for me. I had been through a lot of helpful counseling, but one sentence from God's heart healed decades of pain and hurt and set me free from fear. Experiencing God's love for me enabled me to love myself, brought joy into my life, and transformed me in ways that would take many books to describe. This encounter, this revelation by His Holy Spirit, changed me in areas of my life that I thought would always be broken.

 BECOMING ROOTED

Knowing begins with stillness. *"Be still and know that I am God." (Psalm 46:10)* Consider our tree. It does not run around gathering information about the type of nutrients it needs. It does not go to class after class, memorizing data. The tree has learned the art of stillness. Only in stillness can its roots go deep. Only in stillness can it reach out and touch, feel, and receive all of the nutrients that it needs to grow healthy, tall and strong.

 **PRAYER**

Thank You, God, that You created me to know You. It was never Your intention for me to just know things about You. You have called me into a deep, experiential relationship with You. You want me to feel Your love for me, to experience Your freedom, and to be filled to overflowing with Your tangible presence. Draw near to me, God, as I draw near to You. Meet with me, and change me.

Amen.

REACHING DEEPER

How do we move from knowing about God to this place of encounter? Tomorrow we will walk through an exercise based on Psalm 46 that will begin with what we know in our heads to be true about God and move us toward *Yada*.

> *"I keep asking that the God of our Lord Jesus Christ, the glorious Father, may give you the Spirit of wisdom and revelation, so that you may know Him better."*
> *(Ephesians 1:17)*

WEEK ONE:

DEEPLY ROOTED IN THE CHARACTER OF GOD

WHEN WE REALIZE GOD IS GREATER THAN WE HOPED HE WOULD BE

THURSDAY

 ## AN EXERCISE IN GOING DEEPER

Yesterday, we learned the difference between knowing God and knowing about God. Remember the word *Yada?* We were created for so much more than just having a mental understanding of what God is like. We were created to experience God. We were created to touch Him, to hear Him, and to feel Him.

Sometimes, we need to start with head knowledge. If we are facing a difficult circumstance, we need to know in our heads that God is *good*. We need to have that truth to hang on to. That is where the development of our faith comes into play. The transformation that we need, however, won't come until we have a tangible experience of God's Goodness. This may not always come in a change of our circumstances, but it does always come in an encounter with the true heart of God. This is the gift of revelation.

But how do we get to this place of *Yada*? How do we move from head knowledge to heart knowledge?

Below you will find a list of steps that will help you transition from knowing God to *KNOWING* God based on Psalm 46:10:

"Be still and know that I am God."

 # QUESTIONS/ACTIVITIES

1. Take a moment to consider your present circumstances. What area in your life is most in need of an experiential encounter with God?

_____

_____

_____

_____

_____

2. Return to Appendix #One and reread the list of the Names of God.

3. Which Name of God is needed for your circumstance? Write it here and place it in the blank in the prayers below.

_____

_____

4. Find a space where you can take some time to sit quietly before the Lord.

5. The phrase, *Be still*, in our scripture is the Hebrew word *rapha*, which means "cause yourself to let go" or "let yourself become weak." Pray this *rapha* prayer with me.

Gracious and loving God, I am in need of an encounter with Your _(Name)_. I confess that I cannot make this happen on my own. Thank You that You long for me to experience all that You are. Thank You that I don't have to convince You to meet with me. I just have to ask, and You will come running to me. I just have to seek You, and I will be found by You. I place my circumstances at Your feet, giving You my fear and my hurt. I let go of my need to find a solution or to control this situation, trusting that what is on Your heart for me is far greater than anything I could hope for or imagine.

Amen.

6. What scriptures come to mind when You think about this characteristic of God? Write them here.

_____

_____

_____

_____

_____

7. What Bible characters come to mind that encountered God in this way? Write them here.

_____

_____

_____

_____

8. Think about Jesus, Who is our perfect example of the character of God. What did that characteristic look like in His life?

_____

_____

_____

_____

_____

9. How would your perception of your circumstances change if you had an encounter with the fullness of this aspect of God's character?

_____

_____

_____

_____

_____

10. How would it make you feel differently if you *knew (yada)* God in this way?

_____

_____

_____

_____

11. Imagine yourself walking around being filled with the fullness of God in this way. What do you look like? What is different about you?

_____

_____

_____

_____

_____

"And I pray that you, being rooted and established in love, may have power, together with all the Lord's holy people, to grasp how wide and long and high and deep is the love of Christ, and to know this love that surpasses understanding- that you may be filled to all the fullness of God."
(Ephesians 3:17-19)

 **BECOMING DEEPLY ROOTED**

The difference between head knowledge about God and heart knowledge about God is the difference between life and death. It is the difference between a tree sitting in a parking lot waiting to be sold and a tree planted in nutrient rich soil, receiving all it needs to grow strong and be full of life. As we connect with

Who God is and experience the fullness of His heart for us, we are changed and filled with His powerful life.

 **PRAYER**

Infinite God, what a joy it is to discover new aspects of Who You are. Every Name You declare Yourself to be for me changes me and makes me more like You. Lord, I need to know You more. I need to encounter more of You. Would You reveal Yourself to me as _(Name of God)_? Would You show me what that means in my life? What does that look like? What does that feel like? Cause me to lean into Who You are in my present circumstances. Thank You that it is Your heart's desire to reveal Yourself to me.

Amen.

WEEK ONE

DEEPLY ROOTED IN THE CHARACTER OF GOD

WHEN WE REALIZE GOD IS GREATER THAN WE HOPED HE WOULD BE

*"In seeing God, we will see
everything else clearly for the first time."*
Randy Alcorn

*"For now we see only a reflection as in a mirror;
then we shall see face to face."*
(1 Corinthians 13:12)

FRIDAY

 WHEN WE SEE

I lived in the Pacific Northwest for about ten years. It is a gorgeous part of the country, but has only two main seasons – the rainy season – and August. In between these two seasons, we would experience a lot of fog. It was amazing to watch the fog roll in over the mountains. However, it often made getting to work in the early morning a little difficult. Sometimes I could hardly see past the hood of my car. It would be like driving through soup. I had to creep along, relying purely on memory in order to find my way. As the day went on, though, I would see shafts of light from the sun breaking through as the fog started to burn off. When this happened, I would know that it was going to become a beautiful day. The sun won out, and the skies took on a bright blue hue. By the afternoon, the awe-inspiring mountain views appeared clear and crisp.

This is a lot like our spirits. We all come before the Lord with veils over our faces and hearts, much like trying to drive through fog. These veils can come from our past experiences, what we have been taught or told, or even our own preferences and comfort zones. We grope around in the fog, seeing dimly (1 Cor. 13:12), clinging to what we have experienced or what we have been taught in the past. More often than not, we don't even realize how blind we are and how much there is yet to see. We creep along, following what we hope is the right way to get to where we want to go. It is not until we turn our face to the Son, however, and He burns away the clouds that block our vision, that we can truly see who He is and what He is calling us to.

THE SEEING SERVANT

A beautiful example of this can be found in 2 Kings 6:15-17.

"When the servant of the man of God rose early in the morning and went out, behold, an army with horses and chariots was all around the city. And the servant said, 'Alas, my master! What shall we do?' He said, 'Do not be afraid, for those who are with us are more than those who are with them.' Then Elisha prayed and said 'O Lord, please open his eyes that he may see.' So the Lord opened the eyes of the young man, and he saw, and behold, the mountain was full of horses and chariots of fire all around Elisha."

This is the act of *revelation*. Webster's Dictionary defines revelation as "something revealed by God to humans and an act of revealing or communicating divine truth." In other words, it is an encounter with the heart and nature of God in a way not previously understood – an opening of our eyes. This goes beyond a simple intellectual agreement with a truth. It leads us into an experience with the Lord that results in an ever-deepening relationship with Him. Elisha's servant woke up to some pretty dire circumstances. They were surrounded by a huge army whose sole intent was to kill them. Their death would be sure, swift, and bloody. There was no way out. Then God opened his eyes, and he saw something about God he hadn't even considered. Now bear in mind, the servant had been traveling with Elisha. He knew that God was mighty and powerful. He had seen God do many great miracles and had heard about what God had done through

Abraham, Moses, Joshua, and Elijah. If, before this morning, someone had asked the servant if he thought God was capable of protecting them, I am sure He would have said *yes*. Yet, it is an entirely different and transformational experience, to have God open your eyes and see your enemy surrounded by a vast army of angels with fiery chariots! I imagine his eyes getting wide, his distressed frown slowly turning into a grin, and his fear and despair melting into a bold, confident joy, eager to see what God would to do next.

 ## BECOMING ROOTED

Sunlight is essential to the life of a tree. It uses the light to create energy for it to grow. Have you ever been in a situation where you just couldn't tell which end was up anymore – where you could not see any way through to the other side? Did you notice how your energy tanked during those seasons? Perhaps you even began to experience lethargy or depression. When we are able to see what God is up to in our lives, we are infused with hope and anticipation, and our energy and vitality are restored.

 ## PRAYER

Just as Elisha prayed, I pray, O Lord, please open my eyes so that I may see more clearly Who You are and that I may recognize Your hand at work in my life.

Amen.

REACHING DEEPER

Like the servant, it can be difficult to step back and see what God sees when it feels like the world is closing in around you. Tomorrow, we are going to practice looking for God's perspective in our circumstances.

WEEK ONE

DEEPLY ROOTED IN THE CHARACTER OF GOD

WHEN WE REALIZE GOD IS GREATER THAN WE HOPED HE WOULD BE

SATURDAY

 ## AN EXERCISE IN GOING DEEPER

Yesterday, we read the story about Elisha's servant. We saw how dramatically his perspective of his circumstances changed when he saw what God was up to. Today we are going to break down that process into tangible steps so that you, too, will be able to learn how to see your circumstances through God's eyes.

QUESTIONS/ACTIVITIES

1. Think about your current situation. Name one thing that you need to see from God's perspective. Write that here.

_____

_____

_____

_____

_____

2. Find a quiet place where you can be still *(rapha - cause yourself to let go or let yourself become weak)* and know *(yada - touch, hear, and see)* that He is God. Quiet yourself before Him, and give Him your circumstances.

3. Ask God to open your eyes and show you how He sees your situation.

4. Reread 2 Kings 6:15-17.

5. Imagine yourself as the servant, looking out on your current circumstances. Let God begin to show you what He is up to. Write down what He shows you.

_____

_____

_____

_____

_____

6. We know that God turns everything for our good. What good
   thing could He bring about through this situation? Write it here.

_____

_____

_____

_____

7. Keep bringing this situation back to the Lord to gain more of
   His perspective.

_____

_____

_____

 BECOMING DEEPLY ROOTED

God's perspective will inevitably infuse us with hope and anticipation. God's plans for us are always unbelievably good and better than anything we can imagine. As we learn to see through His eyes, we will be like the servant, moving from despair to wide-eyed, eager excitement for all God has yet to do.

 PRAYER

Amazing Lord, I cannot begin to comprehend the ways that You are, at this moment, working out my circumstances for my good. Open my eyes, Lord. Let me see You moving in my life and in my heart. Reveal to me the God Who is able to do exceedingly, abundantly more than anything I could even dream up. You are an awesome God, and I stand in awe of You!

Amen.

"Now to Him Who is able to do immeasurably more than anything we can ask or imagine, according to His power that is at work within us, to Him be glory in the church and in Christ Jesus throughout all generations, for ever and ever! Amen." (Ephesians 3:20)

WEEK TWO

DEEPLY ROOTED IN THE VOICE OF GOD

WHEN WE RECEIVE THE MESSAGE OUR HEARTS HAVE LONGED TO HEAR

WEEK TWO

DEEPLY ROOTED IN THE VOICE OF GOD

WHEN WE RECEIVE THE MESSAGE OUR HEARTS HAVE LONGED TO HEAR

*"Whenever there is stillness
there is the still, small voice,
God's speaking from the whirlwind,
nature's old song, and dance..."*
Annie Dillard

*"My sheep listen to my voice;
I know them, and they follow me."*
(John 10:27)

MONDAY

 THE SOUND OF GOD

What does God sound like? How do we recognize His voice among all of the messages that come at us throughout our day? Scripture is filled with stories where people encountered the voice of God:

- God spoke during creation. The first recorded spoken words of God created light, planets, oceans, and animals out of nothingness! This is a voice of absolute power!
- The Father spoke over Jesus at His baptism, "This is my son, whom I love; with Him I am well pleased." This is a voice of total, tender love and acceptance!
- The Lord spoke this to the apostle Paul when he was struggling with an ongoing issue: "My grace is sufficient for you, for my power is perfected in weakness." This is a voice of consuming grace!
- Psalm 29 describes the voice of God like this:

"The voice of the LORD is over the waters; the God of glory thunders, the LORD thunders over the mighty water. The voice of the LORD is powerful; the voice of the LORD is majestic. The voice of the LORD breaks the cedars... The voice of the LORD strikes with flashes of lightning. The voice of the LORD shakes the desert...the voice of the LORD twists the oaks and strips the forests bare. And in His temple all cry, "Glory!""

This is a voice of unrivaled majesty!

In 1 Kings 19, Elijah has his own encounter with the voice of God.

ELIJAH HEARS A SOUND

I Kings 19:11-13

> *"The LORD said, 'Go out and stand on the mountain in the*
> *presence of the LORD, for the LORD is about to pass by.'*
> *Then a great and powerful wind tore the mountains apart and*
> *shattered the rocks before the LORD, but the LORD was not*
> *in the wind. After the wind there was an earthquake, but the*
> *LORD was not in the earthquake. After the earthquake came a*
> *fire, but the LORD was not in the fire. And after the fire came*
> *a gentle whisper. When Elijah heard it, he pulled his cloak over*
> *his face and went out and stood at the mouth of the cave."*

How is it that a voice that brings creation into being, that rattles the earth and thunders over the waters can come to us as a gentle whisper? Many Christians believe they have never heard God speak. They believe that hearing God is reserved for pastors, missionaries, or a rare and special few. But what if, while we are listening for thunder and earthquakes and fire, God is currently and continually whispering gently to our hearts? What if while we are waiting for a booming voice that is more easily heard than the chaos of the world around us, God is waiting for us to quiet our minds and our hearts so that we can hear Him? What if He is waiting for us to BE STILL and KNOW (Yada...touch, feel, experience, **hear**) that He is God? (Psalm 46:10)

BECOMING ROOTED

Did you know that plants respond to sound vibrations? The right sound vibrations can help a plant grow and even strengthen its immune system! Whether it is God's comforting words, His declaration of majesty, or His balm of grace amid trying times, when we hear God's voice, it resonates through our hearts and gives us guidance, strength, and encouragement.

 # PRAYER

Almighty God, Who, with the sound of Your voice, creates life out of nothing; and Who, like with Lazarus, speaks and raises the dead, help me to quiet my heart and mind to hear You. Thank You that, even now, You are speaking to me. Cause me to be still so that I can recognize Your whisper. You are The Living Word, and each word You speak breathes life into me. So speak, LORD. I am listening.

Amen.

 # REACHING DEEPER

Tomorrow we are going to go through a simple practical process of learning how to recognize God's voice. I believe this is one of the most important keys to being able to grow in our relationship with God. It is when we learn how to recognize His voice that we can learn how to follow Him.

"My sheep listen to my voice; I know them, and they follow me."
(John 10:27)

WEEK TWO

DEEPLY ROOTED IN THE VOICE OF GOD

WHEN WE RECEIVE THE MESSAGE OUR HEARTS HAVE LONGED TO HEAR

TUESDAY

 ### AN EXERCISE IN GOING DEEPER

"My sheep hear my voice. I know them and they follow me."
(John 10:27)

You were created to hear the voice of God. Let me say that one more time.

You were created to hear the voice of God.

Do you realize what Satan's first words to humans were? You may recall Adam and Eve and the serpent in the garden – and think, like most of us, that it was him telling them to eat of the forbidden fruit. That is not where it started. The first thing the serpent said to them was, "Did God really say...?" Satan's first act on earth was not to get us to openly sin, but to get us to doubt what we heard from God! In fact, he wants us to doubt that we can hear Him speak to us at all! Friends, if you are in Christ, *you can hear Him speak*, and not just by reading words in the Bible, but through the power of the Holy Spirit within you, bringing Truth and Life to those words and teaching you all things. (John 14:26)

Thousands of voices, opinions, and messages come at us every day. We have become so used to being inundated with information that we feel lost without it. Just look around at how many of us live our lives with our phones in our hands. No wonder we can find it difficult to hear God's voice! Listening takes practice. Being still requires a different set of muscles than we are used to using in our society.

Last week when we were learning about the character of God, we started by determining where we were in our journey. We began by finding the "You are here" sticker on the map. Today, we are going to begin this process in the same way and build on it throughout the rest of the week.

You may be surprised to discover how much God has already been speaking to you throughout your life.

 # QUESTIONS/ACTIVITIES

1. It is always helpful to start from a place of stillness (*rapha - cause yourself to let go or let yourself become weak*). Find a

quiet place, and give all of your thoughts and concerns over to the Lord.

2. Ask God to show you the ways He has been leading, guiding, and speaking to you.

3. Here are some common ways that God speaks to us.

   a. Feeling an *inner nudge* to call someone up on the phone to check on them.

   b. Listening to a sermon and feeling like it was spoken just to you.

   c. Reading a passage of scripture and feeling like it just wrapped around your heart and gave you just what you needed.

   d. Having a verse or Bible story pop into your head that connects to a situation you are facing.

   e. Experiencing inexplicable peace or comfort in the middle of a difficult situation.

   f. Having a person come up to you and encourage you just when you needed it.

   g. Noticing a common theme in your conversations that draws you to the heart of God.

   h. Feeling drawn to worship, prayer, or time in the Word.

i. Feeling compassion for someone that you know is beyond your own compassion.

4. Write down any experiences you have had with the voice of God in light of these examples.

_____

_____

_____

_____

_____

 **BECOMING DEEPLY ROOTED**

Like the plant that responds to specific sound waves in order to grow stronger and healthier, this exercise has helped you tune into God's sound wave over you. As you learn to recognize what His voice sounds like, you will come to discover the amazing truth that God is always speaking. He is always at work in your life, and He is always guiding, encouraging, and strengthening you as you continue to grow in your relationship with Him.

 **PRAYER**

Lord, thank You for the many ways You speak to me. Thank You that it is Your promise that I can hear and recognize Your voice. Thank You that You still whisper to my heart. You still nudge me, direct me, and teach me. I am so grateful for Your voice. Help me to hear You more clearly.

Amen.

WEEK TWO

DEEPLY ROOTED IN THE VOICE OF GOD

WHEN WE RECEIVE THE MESSAGE OUR HEARTS HAVE LONGED TO HEAR

"To meditate on Scripture is to allow the truth of God's word to move from head to heart. It is to so dwell upon a truth that it becomes part of our being."
Greg Ogden

"In the beginning was the Word,
and the Word was with God,
and the Word was God."
(John 1:1)

WEDNESDAY

 HEARING GOD'S VOICE IN SCRIPTURE

If you want to learn how to hear God's voice more clearly, there is no better place to start than in the Word. Scripture has been given to us so that we may know the loving heart of God. When we approach scripture, we must come humbly and open to receive what God wants to show us. God has given us, not only this beautiful gift of His Word in which to know Him better, but He has also blessed us with the Holy Spirit to teach us and remind us of all that Christ has shown us. Think about this for a moment. When we approach scripture, we get to read the Word of God with The Living Word!

 WHEN THE LIVING WORD READ THE WORD TO ME

One of the first things I clearly heard the Holy Spirit speak to me was "Psalm 27 is for you." I had no idea at the time what psalm 27 was or what it said, so of course, I was curious. Opening my Bible, I wondered if I was going to come upon some obscure passage that meant nothing to me and would validate my doubts about my ability to hear Him, but that wasn't the case. I was pleasantly surprised at what I found in Psalm 27 – several familiar passages that God had used in my life over the years.

Psalm 27

¹ The Lord is my light and my salvation—
whom shall I fear?
The Lord is the stronghold of my life—
of whom shall I be afraid?

² When the wicked advance against me
to devour[a] me,
it is my enemies and my foes
who will stumble and fall.
³ Though an army besiege me,
my heart will not fear;
though war break out against me,
even then I will be confident.

⁴ One thing I ask from the Lord,
this only do I seek:
that I may dwell in the house of the Lord
all the days of my life,
to gaze on the beauty of the Lord
and to seek him in his temple.
⁵ For in the day of trouble
he will keep me safe in his dwelling;
he will hide me in the shelter of his sacred tent
and set me high upon a rock.

⁶ Then my head will be exalted
above the enemies who surround me;
at his sacred tent I will sacrifice with shouts of joy;
I will sing and make music to the Lord.

⁷ Hear my voice when I call, Lord;
be merciful to me and answer me.
⁸ My heart says of you, "Seek his face!"
Your face, Lord, I will seek.
⁹ Do not hide your face from me,
do not turn your servant away in anger;
God my Savior.
¹⁰ Though my father and mother forsake me,
the Lord will receive me.
¹¹ Teach me your way, Lord;
lead me in a straight path
because of my oppressors.
¹² Do not turn me over to the desire of my foes,
for false witnesses rise up against me,
spouting malicious accusations.

¹³ I remain confident of this:
I will see the goodness of the Lord
in the land of the living.
¹⁴ Wait for the Lord;
be strong and take heart
and wait for the Lord.

What a treasure trove of riches it was – and still is! From speaking "The LORD is the stronghold of my life – of whom shall I be afraid?" coming from a girl so fearful and insecure, I barely spoke – to, "One thing I ask from the LORD, this only do I seek: that I may dwell in the house of the LORD all the days of my life, to gaze on the beauty of the LORD and to seek Him in His temple." This verse is still the deepest cry of my heart and the verse that my spirit calls out to God with on a regular basis. From the words, "He will keep me safe in His dwelling," spoken by a girl that had known much hurt – to, "Teach me your way, LORD," which has been my cry for guidance and direction when the way seemed clouded and confusing. This chapter from Psalms gave me a promise to stand on, "I remain confident of this: I will see the goodness of the LORD in the land of the living," when everything else seemed dark and hopeless around me, and it brought a word of encouragement to my soul when I was weary. "Wait for the LORD; be strong and take heart and wait for the LORD."

This scripture has been with me – in my heart, in my spirit, and in my mind – for decades. The Holy Spirit never ceases to use it to remind me of Who God is for me, to pick me up and brush me off when I have fallen, to speak God's love and protection over me, and to draw me deeper into His heart. It is a scripture He brought to life for me, and it is my inheritance from Him.

Jesus spoke a scripture from the Old Testament that He adopted as His own. When He went into the synagogue in Nazareth, his home town, according to Luke 4:16-21, "*He stood up to read, and the scroll of the prophet Isaiah was handed to him. Unrolling it, he found the place where it is written: 'The Spirit of the Lord is on me, because He has anointed me to proclaim good news to the poor. He has sent me to proclaim freedom for the prisoners and recovery of sight for the blind, to set the oppressed free, and to proclaim the year of the Lord's favor.' (Isaiah 61:1-2). Then He rolled up the scroll, gave it back to the attendant and sat down. The eyes of everyone in the synagogue were fastened on Him. He began by saying to them, 'Today this scripture is fulfilled in your hearing.'*"

What an amazing moment! The scripture that they had studied, memorized, and all known so well, came to life before their eyes in the person of Jesus! It was His inheritance given to Him by His Father, and He spoke it out, proclaimed it, and lived it.

What if the Holy Spirit is waiting to captivate your heart with His Word? What if He wants you to not only understand what it says, but also have an encounter with Him as you read it, hear it, and meditate on it? What treasures, promises, and encouragements could be there just waiting for you? What comfort, direction, and freedom could you find?

 # BECOMING ROOTED

Scripture has often compared the Word of God to being our daily bread. It nourishes us. It sustains us. Like nutrients in the soil to a tree, the word of God feeds us and gives us life. But a tree does not just spend 15 minutes a day scanning over the soil. A tree dwells in the soil. It soaks in the nutrients until it is filled. So we also have the gift to dwell in the Word. This does not mean going on a scripture reading marathon and seeing how much we can read in a sitting. What this does mean is that we get to soak in the Word, meditate on it, and let it fill us. We may find that God wants to share with us His heart in one passage that we continue to contemplate on for months, so that it goes deep within us and we are fundamentally changed by it. It is a deep and beautiful process that transforms us and makes us rich in Christ.

 # PRAYER

Lord, Your Word is life because You are life. Burn in me a hunger for Your Word. Cause Your Spirit to wrap Your Word around my heart. Take me to the scriptures that speak to me and that draw me closer to You. Share Your promises with me, and reveal to me more of Who You are through Your written Word.

Amen.

 # REACHING DEEPER

Many of us never learned what it means to dwell in the Word. I went to a Christian school growing up, and for me, between Bible classes and Sunday school, the Bible became a book of information about God to memorize and be tested on. I had gone through many "read the Bible in one year" studies, and learned a lot about the history, time-lines, and geography of Biblical stories. What I didn't learn until much later in life was how to slow down and soak in the Word of God. I didn't know how to live there and find deep nourishment from it. Tomorrow, we will go through an exercise of learning how to dwell in the Word and how to let the Word dwell in us.

"Let the Word of God dwell in you richly."
(Colossians 3:16)

WEEK TWO

DEEPLY ROOTED IN THE VOICE OF GOD

WHEN WE RECEIVE THE MESSAGE OUR HEARTS HAVE LONGED TO HEAR

THURSDAY

 ## AN EXERCISE IN GOING DEEPER

"In the beginning was the Word, and the Word was with God, and the Word was God."
(John 1:1)

Long before pen was put to paper, and ages before the Bible was ever compiled, was The Word. When we open our Bibles and engage scripture by the guidance and power of the Holy Spirit, we are not just reading verses; we are dwelling with The Word by His

Holy Spirit. What an amazing way to encounter and know God better! It's not just by memorizing passages and gaining more intellectual understanding of the Bible, but by opening the Word in the presence of The Living Word. It's by submitting ourselves to Him to receive life and power and freedom through those words penned by His Spirit so long ago!

Today, we will be going through an exercise of learning how to read scripture while having our hearts open to listen to what the Holy Spirit wants to say to us through the Word. We will be using Psalm 23 as an example to start from.

Psalm 23

¹ The LORD is my shepherd, I lack nothing.
² He makes me lie down in green pastures,
he leads me beside quiet waters,
³ he refreshes my soul.
He guides me along the right paths
For his name's sake.
⁴ Even though I walk through the darkest valley,
I will fear no evil,
for you are with me;
your rod and your staff, they comfort me.
⁵ You prepare a table before me
In the presence of my enemies.
You anoint my head with oil;
My cup overflows.
⁶ Surely your goodness and love will follow me
All the days of my life,
And I will dwell in the house of the LORD
Forever.

QUESTIONS/ACTIVITIES

1. Find a quiet place where you can be still before the Lord.

2. *Rapha (to let go and become weak).* Let go of everything you thought you knew about this Psalm. It may be helpful to use a different translation than you are used to in order to gain a fresh perspective, especially if it is a passage you have heard many times.

3. Ask God to sit next to you and read the passage with you.

4. Ask Him to open your eyes so that you can see this passage afresh.

5. Ask Him to speak to you and to show you what this passage means for you in your life.

6. SLOWLY read through this passage. Take your time. Meditate on the meaning of each word and phrase.

7. SLOWLY read through this passage a second time. Write down the promises that God has for you in this chapter. (For example, in verse 1, God promises that He will provide everything you need.)

_____

_____

_____

_____

_____

8. Let God speak into your life through this scripture. What else is He showing you? Write it here.

_____

_____

_____

_____

9. If you want to take this one step deeper, rewrite this passage in your own words, thinking through your own circumstances.

_____

_____

_____

_____

10. Come back to this passage again and again until David's words become your own, and God's Word dwells in you richly.

 BECOMING DEEPLY ROOTED

Keep a list of verses, passages, or promises from God's Word that give you strength, comfort, and encouragement. As you study the Word, go through this process with those scriptures. You will find that this list grows as you learn to dwell in His Word and let His Word richly fill your heart and spirit.

 **PRAYER**

Lord, thank You that no matter how I am feeling or what my circumstances are telling me, I can rely on Your Word. I trust that Your promises are true because You are trustworthy. Thank You that there is no end to the ways in which You reveal Yourself to me through Your Word, because it is still living and active in my life. Open my heart even more to receive all that You have for me in Your scriptures.

Amen.

WEEK TWO

DEEPLY ROOTED IN THE VOICE OF GOD

WHEN WE RECEIVE THE MESSAGE OUR HEARTS HAVE LONGED TO HEAR

"He whispered
And I leaned towards Him.
That's what He wanted.
Me.
Closer."
When God Speaks by F. Farai

"But when He, the Spirit of truth, comes, He will guide you
into all truth. He will not speak on His own; He will speak
only what He hears, and He will tell you what is yet to come.
He will glorify me because it is from me that He will receive
what He will make known to you."
(John 16:13-14)

"In the last days, God says, I will pour out my Spirit on all people. Your sons and daughters will prophesy, your young men will see visions, your old men will dream dreams. Even on my servants, both men and women, I will pour out my Spirit in those days, and they will prophesy."
(Acts 2:17-18)

FRIDAY

 ## LISTENING TO THE VOICE OF THE HOLY SPIRIT

Jesus sent His Holy Spirit to us in order to teach us, guide us, and point us to Christ. The Bible is FULL of countless ways that God speaks to His children. Just a few examples include:

- Scripture: (Example: In Acts 2, the Holy Spirit is talking to and through Peter about Joel 2, Psalm 16, and Psalm 110, all in the same conversation!)
- An inner nudging: (Example: Acts 15:28 states, "It seemed right to the Holy Spirit and to us.")
- Images/visions (Example: In Acts 10:9-16, Peter has a vision in which God is showing him that salvation is not just for Jews, but for everyone.)
- Dreams (Examples: Genesis 37, Matthew 1, Matthew 27, Acts 2:17-18)
- A gentle whisper. (I Kings 19:12-13)

- A word or phrase coming to mind from seemingly out of nowhere.
- Noticing a repeated theme in conversations or throughout your day.
- Feeling drawn to a particular scripture.
- Feeling drawn to check in on someone or pray for them.
- Experiencing a sense of peace about something.

Keep in mind that hearing an audible voice from the Lord or having what some call *an open vision*, meaning that it is a vision you see more clearly than what is actually, tangibly in front of your face, are rare occurrences. God speaks to us because He wants to draw us deeper into conversation and into relationship with Him. He whispers because it causes us to move closer to Him in order to hear Him. Most often, it requires a level of faith and trust to believe that you actually heard from the Lord.

Everyone is created uniquely by the Father, and He will have a unique way of speaking to each of us. It is a joyful adventure as we get to discover the ways He speaks to us as our relationship with Him grows stronger.

I know people who hear God's voice providing wisdom and guiding them in their business decisions, so that they can be a source of provision to those around them. I know someone who gets up in the morning and asks God to show him what to put in his backpack before he walks across a homeless camp on the way to work. He inevitably meets people who are in desperate need of what he packed that morning, and God uses him to spread the Gospel to those in need. I know people who hear God's voice in songs, people who can feel what is going on in the hearts of those around them, people who experience a physical sensation in a part of their body when God wants them to pray for healing for someone, people who are given words of encouragement for others and have a ministry of writing and sending notes to those who need to be lifted up, people who hear God's heart for organizations and churches and listen to God's strategies for those places, and even people who God speaks to in colors. Intercessors, many times, hear God's heart about a particular location, neighborhood, or city, and pray from that place with authority. The different ways God speaks to us are as creative and unique as we are. God gives each of us a way to express His heart that no one else can!

A number of years ago I was going through a particularly long season where I felt very distant from God. I had been crying out to God about it, feeling kind of lost and very confused. One night, He answered my prayers by giving me a dream:

 # MY DREAM FROM GOD

I was surrounded by darkness, and out of the darkness a voice thundered, "Behold, the Lion of the tribe of Judah!" Then I was suddenly surrounded by a huge crowd of people all looking in the same direction. I turned my head and saw a huge Lion slowly moving along the road. He was crouched and seemed to be stalking prey. Then I noticed that He was covered in blood, deep wounds, and large gashes. At first, I assumed He was walking like that because He must have been in a tremendous amount of pain. I then realized the real reason this majestic Lion was walking so slowly and low to the ground was that a small girl was asleep on His back, and He didn't want to wake her! She was in a place of utter love, peace, and protection and didn't even realize it! The entire crowd grew completely still and silent in the presence of such Holy

Tenderness. I began to feel as if I didn't deserve to be there. I felt heavy under the weight of such Glory and Majesty passing before me. I just couldn't turn my eyes away. Then, all of a sudden, the Lion – this Holy and Awesome Being, turned and looked straight at me. His eyes pierced my heart. I sucked in a breath, and then, the most unexpected thing happened! The Lion's eyes lit up, and He gave me a huge, toothy smile, and *waved* at me! He acted like a child who had just spotted his best friend across the playground! The childlike joy He expressed at seeing me in the midst of such a holy moment left me utterly undone! I began weeping uncontrollably and woke up with tears streaming down my cheeks. In fact, the dream impacted me so much, that I continued to weep for days, out of love for Him!

I had gone to bed feeling so distant from Him, and I woke up knowing His heart so much more! Like the familiar story about the footsteps in the sand, He wasn't distant from me – He was carrying me on His back so that I could rest in Him! I had encountered His delight, His joy, and His love over me in a way I had not experienced before, and it changed me forever!

This is why Jesus sent the Holy Spirit to us – to lead us into all truth and to glorify Christ. His Spirit, that is now living in every person who has put their trust in Jesus, is continually revealing to us more about what Christ is like. He is currently at work teaching us, guiding us, and helping us. In fact, John 14:26 names Him *the Helper.*

 # BECOMING ROOTED

Real growth takes time. The roots need to dig in and expand in order to support the tree as it grows. There is no simple formula for being able to hear God's voice. It takes time and practice. He rarely speaks in the exact same way twice. God whispers because it draws us closer to Him. That is what He longs for. He draws us into conversation so that we might go deeper into relationship with Him. He wants to bring us into stillness so that He can speak tenderly to us. This is how our spiritual roots grow deep and secure, so that in seasons of turmoil we are not uprooted from our relationship with Him

 **PRAYER**

Jesus, what an amazing gift You have given me in the Holy Spirit! Thank You that You did not leave me alone, but gave me just Who I needed. Help me be more aware of Your presence in me and where You, through Your Holy Spirit, are at work in and around me. Help me become more sensitive to the voice of Your Spirit and the many ways You speak to me. Open my eyes to see and my ears to hear what the Holy Spirit is showing me.

Amen.

 REACHING DEEPER

Tomorrow, we will learn how to position ourselves near God and stay there so that we can hear His whispers. We will learn how to distinguish His voice from the noise around us, and we will practice stepping out in faith with what He speaks.

WEEK TWO

DEEPLY ROOTED IN THE VOICE OF GOD

*WHEN WE RECEIVE THE
MESSAGE OUR HEARTS
HAVE LONGED TO HEAR*

SATURDAY

 ## AN EXERCISE IN GOING DEEPER

Yesterday we discovered countless ways in which God speaks to us, and He delights in speaking to us and sharing His heart with us. We learned that everyone who has given their life to Christ has the Holy Spirit living in them, and has the ability to hear God's voice. Throughout the exercises this week, we began to practice listening to God's voice and learning what His voice sounds like.

Today we are going to take the next step in practicing listening to the Holy Spirit and becoming more sensitive to the Spirit's voice and leading in our lives.

QUESTIONS/ACTIVITIES

Things to keep in mind as you go through this process:

When you have a thought come to you that you think may be from God, check what you heard against the Word and the Holy Spirit. Make sure it doesn't go against scripture, and check the fruit. Is it undergirded by love, joy, peace, patience, kindness, or another fruit of the spirit, or does it leave you feeling anxious, judgmental, condemned, frustrated, or discouraged? If you are truly seeking to draw closer to God, you will find that even conviction from the Holy Spirit leaves you feeling loved, excited, and hopeful as He is making you more like Christ. The Holy Spirit truly is the most encouraging person I have ever met! As you continue to have encounters with the heart of God for you and others, you will more easily recognize His voice and be able to distinguish it from all the other voices that shout at you every moment of every day.

1. Take a moment to consider something you would like to talk about with Jesus. Write that down here.

_____

_____

_____

_____

_____

2. Take a few minutes to praise Him for Who He is, and thank Him for all He has done. Worship is a great practical act of *rapha –letting go.* It lifts us above our circumstances and places us in God's presence where we can see things from His perspective. Write down any shift you experience in how you feel about your situation.

_____

_____

_____

_____

_____

3. Find a place to quiet yourself and be still before the Lord.

4. Take five to ten minutes to just listen. Write down anything that comes to mind. It doesn't matter if you are not 100% sure if what comes to your mind is from God. We will come back to this list later to check what you have heard against scripture and the fruit of the Spirit.

_____

_____

_____

_____

_____

5. Ask God to show you His perspective on your situation. Write down what He shows you.

_____

_____

_____

_____

6. Write down any scripture verses that come to mind.

_____

_____

_____

_____

_____

7. Write down any promises that He gives you.

_____

_____

_____

_____

_____

8. Ask Him to show you how He wants to make you more like Him in this season.

_____

_____

_____

_____

_____

9. Ask Him if there is something that He would have you do or change.

_____

_____

_____

_____

_____

10. Ask God to show you anything else He would like to share with you about your situation, and take five more minutes to just listen and write down whatever comes to mind.

_____

_____

_____

_____

11. Go back through the things that you wrote in questions 4-10. Is there anything that goes against scripture or the fruit of the Spirit? If so, cross those things out.

12. Now look through the remainder of the things that you wrote in Questions 4-10. Is there something that God is bringing to your attention? It may be a scripture. It may be just a word or a feeling. It does not need to be long or complex. The most powerful thing I ever heard from God was, "I just love you so much!" It may be a word that doesn't make a lot of sense to you right now, but you are feeling

drawn to exploring it further with God. Write those things here.

_____

_____

_____

_____

13. If you hear something that you believe may be from God, and it passes the *checks*, take a risk, and step out in faith! Start with small risks. If you feel like God has put someone on your heart to call, call them and see where it leads. If you have a thought to send a note of encouragement to someone, send it! When we are faithful with small things, God will be able to trust us with more. Write down your step of faith and your experiences here.

_____

_____

_____

_____

*Important note: You may not have felt like you heard anything, and that is okay. God brings us through different seasons. If you don't hear anything, just sit quietly with Him. Those can be very powerful times! Trust that you will hear Him eventually. In the meantime, like the little girl on the back of the Lion, find peace and rest in knowing that He is with you, and that He loves you deeply.

BECOMING DEEPLY ROOTED

This is where the conversation of a lifetime begins! Take these things back before the Lord on a regular basis, as He directs you. Ask Him to show you more. Ask Him to expand that word into a sentence. Ask Him how He would like you to respond – and then respond in that way. Keep track of all the additional things God shows you in the coming weeks and months about this situation. You will find that, instead of just waiting for a simple *yes* or *no* answer to a prayer request, entering into an ongoing conversation with God will draw you into a deeper and more powerful relationship with Him. You will come away with a life-changing revelation of God's heart for you. You will grow in understanding the way He thinks and moves. You will also see more clearly His perspective of your circumstances, as well as the future plans He has for you that you cannot even imagine right now!

 **PRAYER**

God, thank You for Your voice. Thank You that it is Your deepest desire to speak to me, to show me how You see me, to show me what You are like, and to show me how much You love me. Thank You for drawing me deeper into relationship with You, so that I can experience how truly good You are and how amazing Your plans are for me. Open my ears to hear You, Lord. Help me be attentive to the many ways You are speaking to me. Thank You that You are with me, and You will never leave me.

Amen.

WEEK THREE

DEEPLY ROOTED IN THE PROMISES OF GOD

WHEN WE FIND OURSELVES STANDING ON AN UNSHAKABLE FOUNDATION

WEEK THREE

DEEPLY ROOTED IN THE PROMISES OF GOD

WHEN WE FIND OURSELVES STANDING ON AN UNSHAKABLE FOUNDATION

> *"God never made a promise that was too good to be true."*
> *Dwight L. Moody*

"For no matter how many promises God has made, they are 'Yes' in Christ. And so through Him the 'Amen' is spoken by us to the glory of God."
(2 Cor. 1:20)

MONDAY

 ## GOD IS A KEEPER OF PROMISES

From the beginning, God has declared His heart, His intentions, and His promises to His people.

Has anyone ever broken a promise to you? Perhaps a parent promised to show up for your game or recital, but did not make it. Perhaps you have been through a divorce or experienced a betrayal. Maybe someone wasn't there for you when you needed them to be. These types of experiences can strongly impact our ability to trust. We have been let down. We have been hurt, and we double our defenses to make sure that it doesn't happen again. Many of us have even found ourselves angry at God. "If there is a God, why would He let something like this happen?" There is an overwhelming amount of needless cruelty and suffering in the world. Evil throws itself in our faces on a daily basis, and we have no idea how to make sense of it. The truth is, there is no easy answer.

What we can be sure of, though, is God's loving faithfulness. He took on our sorrows and sufferings on the cross. He understands the pain we feel. He weeps when we weep. He is not the creator of evil. He has, in fact, given His life so that we do not have to carry the consequences of evil around with us.

We can also confidently lean on the thousands of promises that God has given us through scripture. That is a LOT of GOOD NEWS for us to cling to! God has been so generous to give us more promises than we can hold, for every difficulty we face.

Instead of being overwhelmed by our circumstances, we can be overwhelmed by God's Goodness and the Promises He has for us.

In a world of broken promises and destroyed trust, and in a world that provokes fear and defensiveness, we have another option. We have a God Who is consistently Good and Faithful. We have His Word that is trustworthy and true. In addition to that, we have His promises that are all *yes* for us through Christ.

 # AN UNBROKEN PROMISE

In fact, God is so faithful to keep His promises that we don't even need to be aware that He made them. He will still be true to His Word. Growing up, I was incredibly withdrawn. I barely spoke and had very few friends. My best friend was Jesus. He was my only playmate. We would walk in the woods together, play "fort" together, and sing together. He was often the only person I spoke to, and the only one who actually saw me for who I was. I remember begging Jesus to come into my heart every day. I was so afraid that He would leave me and I would be all alone. As I got older, I grew to understand that He made a promise to never leave me. I began to grow in peace and trust that He would always be there with me, no matter what, and after forty-some years of life's ups and downs, that remains a promise kept.

 # BECOMING ROOTED

I live about a mile from Lake Michigan. The shores near me are made of tall sand dunes. Every year, the dunes erode a little more. It has reached the point where roads are being lost and many houses are in danger. They have tried to plant grasses and plants in the sand to prevent erosion and loss of property, but it hasn't worked as well as they hoped. Sand shifts. It is not stable ground for roots to dig in and grow. When storms blow in, the plants blow over. Plants need stable soil in which to grow. So do we. The promises of God are firm and secure ground where we can stand. When the storms of life blow in, they do not shift or erode beneath us. We can trust that God will keep His Word, and we will not be shaken.

 **PRAYER**

Father, thank You that I can trust You to always keep your promises to me. Thank You that I can rely on You and stand firm in Your love. Show me the promises You have given me, and through them, reveal to me more of Your heart.

Amen.

 **REACHING DEEPER**

Tomorrow, we will be taking a deeper look at some of the countless promises God has given us.

WEEK THREE

DEEPLY ROOTED IN THE PROMISES OF GOD

WHEN WE FIND OURSELVES STANDING ON AN UNSHAKABLE FOUNDATION

TUESDAY

AN EXERCISE IN GOING DEEPER

Yesterday we learned that we can always trust God to keep His promises. But what are His promises? Biblical scholars estimate that there are as many as three thousand promises to be found in God's Word! That is an abundance of promises to stand on for every situation you may face!

Today we will be starting in the same place we have for the last two weeks. We will be finding the "You are here" sticker on our trail map by taking a look at some of the many promises God has given us.

 # QUESTIONS/ACTIVITIES

1. In the back of this book, I have created a list of some of the many promises of God. Turn to Appendix #Two and take some time to look them over. Slowly read through them, and consider the truth in them. Again, I highly recommend that you read this list out loud. Something powerful happens when we speak out God's promises over ourselves.

2. Pray and ask God to show you ways in which He has kept His promises to you.

3. Look through the list again, and think about a time when God kept one of these promises to you. Write down the story here.

_____

_____

_____

_____

4. Thank God for always being faithful to keep His promises.

BECOMING DEEPLY ROOTED

We become deeply rooted in the promises of God for us as we learn to let His promises fill us and sustain us. The more we stand on His Word, the more we learn to trust that He is faithful to keep His Word. Pick one of the promises from the list, and write it in a place that you will see it throughout the week. Keep declaring that promise over yourself, and ask God to open your eyes to see the many ways that He is faithful to keep that promise to you. Write down the moments that you noticed His faithfulness to that promise this week.

PRAYER

God, thank You for Your abundant promises that will never fail. Cause me, in the midst of my circumstances, to rise up and stand firmly on Who You are and what You say You will do.

Amen.

WEEK THREE

DEEPLY ROOTED IN THE PROMISES OF GOD

WHEN WE FIND OURSELVES STANDING ON AN UNSHAKABLE FOUNDATION

*"Let God's promises shine
on your problems."*
Corrie ten Boom

"Everything that goes into a life of pleasing God has been miraculously given to us by getting to know, personally and intimately, the One who invited us to God. The best invitation we ever received! We were also given absolutely terrific promises to pass on to you - your tickets to participation in the life of God."
(2 Peter 1:3-4, The Message)

WEDNESDAY

 ## A FIRM FOUNDATION

God's promises are given to us so that we have a firm place to stand in the midst of a crisis. One of my heroes is Corrie ten Boom. As a Christian during WWII, Corrie and her family began hiding Jews in their home. Eventually, Corrie and her family were caught and sent to a Nazi concentration camp, where she shared her faith with the guards and prisoners there. Her biography, *The Hiding Place*, is a gripping tale of unshakable faith in the midst of unimaginable suffering. Her quote "Let God's promises shine on your problems," in light of all that she endured, speaks of a God that can bring good out of truly anything. It speaks of a sure foundation in the promises of God that can weather any storm.

 ## ADRIFT IN A STORM

Imagine you are out in the ocean where a big storm is brewing. The sky is turning dark. The water is churning around you. The waves are crashing over you, pulling you deeper and deeper under the current. You are flailing about, trying to keep your head up, but the current is getting too strong, and you are growing weak and tired. Suddenly, you spot a life boat. It takes all the energy you have left, but you make your way toward it. Grabbing on tight, you begin to pull yourself up. As you get your body over the side, all your muscles relax. You catch your breath and begin to find warmth in the safety of the boat. The storm is still raging around you, but you are secure. Now, all you need to do is just wait it out.

This is what a promise from God is like for us in the middle of life's circumstances. Sometimes we find ourselves surrounded by struggles. Perhaps it is an illness, a broken relationship, or financial difficulties. We try so hard to fix the problem, or at least keep our head above water. We work and fight and flail about, but only seem to take on more weariness and discouragement. The amazing thing is that God has a promise for you in the middle of your situation. He has promised to turn everything around for your good – EVERYTHING! Now, you get to discover what that *good* is. In order to discover the promise for you, though, you need to stop fighting your circumstances and look up. Just like the life boat, the promise is there if you just look for it. Once you discover the promise in God's Word, put your energy into grabbing hold of it. Meditate on it. Pray about it. Thank God for it. Declare it out loud to yourself. When you feel the waves crashing against you, anxiety rising, or discouragement setting in, hold on tighter. As you do, your spiritual muscles become stronger until you are able to pull yourself up and find rest and security in God's promise for you. As you learn to stand on these promises, you will rise above your circumstances and dwell in God's joy, peace, and rest.

 # BECOMING ROOTED

As we learn to practice holding on to God's promises for us in the midst of life's storms, our roots grow deeper into God. We become strong and unshakable as we learn to stand on the strong and unshakable Word of God.

 **PRAYER**

Dear God, thank You for Your many promises. Thank You that I don't have to wonder if they are for me. You say *yes* to all of them for my life, and You are at work in bringing them to fruition for me. Thank You that I can trust Your Word and Your love for me. Help me find peace and rest in Your promises and in Your heart for me.

Amen.

 **REACHING DEEPER**

Tomorrow, we will go through a simple exercise in learning how to discover and hold onto God's promises amid our circumstances.

WEEK THREE

DEEPLY ROOTED IN THE PROMISES OF GOD

WHEN WE FIND OURSELVES STANDING ON AN UNSHAKABLE FOUNDATION

THURSDAY

 ## AN EXERCISE IN GOING DEEPER

Yesterday, we learned about the unshakable promises of God. These promises provide a safe and secure place to stand, no matter how difficult our circumstances are.

Today we are going to go through a simple exercise in learning how to discover God's promises for us, how to grab hold of those promises, and how to find a place of hope and rest as we stand on God's Word.

QUESTIONS/ACTIVITIES

1. Return to the list of God's promises in Appendix #Two at the back of the book.

2. Find a quiet place where you can be still (*remember the word, rapha – to let go, become weak?*) and know (*remember the word, yada – to touch, feel, experience?*) that He is God.

3. Think about your current circumstances. Write down one situation in which you need a breakthrough from God.

_____

_____

_____

_____

_____

4. Ask God to show you how He sees your situation. (You may want to refer back to our exercises from Week Two where we first learned how to hear God's voice. This is going to be an important aspect in our ongoing adventure with Him!) Write down what He shows you.

_____

_____

_____

_____

_____

5. Now, read out loud through the list of promises in Appendix #Two.

6. Choose one promise that God highlights for you and your situation. Write it here and place it in the blank in the prayer below.

_____

_____

_____

_____

_____

7. Write down this promise and place it somewhere you will see it throughout your day. Take time to memorize it.

BECOMING DEEPLY ROOTED

As we practice holding on to God's promises for us, we are changed by His Word. Whenever you find yourself worrying about that circumstance, every time a situation comes up that puts your problem back on your heart, declare God's promise over yourself. Remind yourself what He said to you. Remember that Satan likes to get us to doubt what God has said. That is why we write it down and keep His Word in front of us. After you have reminded yourself of God's promise, pray the prayer below. You will find your heart changing, the more you do this. You will find yourself guarded by God's peace and strengthened by His Word.

PRAYER

Thank you God, that you have promised ___(promise)___. Thank you that I can trust Your Word to be true. I choose to rest on your promises instead of becoming discouraged, frustrated, or anxious about my circumstances.

Amen.

WEEK THREE

DEEPLY ROOTED IN THE PROMISES OF GOD

WHEN WE FIND OURSELVES STANDING ON AN UNSHAKABLE FOUNDATION

"We like to control the map of our life and know everything well in advance. But faith is content just knowing that God's promise cannot fail. This, in fact, is the excitement of walking with God."
Jim Cymbala

"Trust in the Lord with all your heart and lean not on your own understanding; in all your ways submit to Him, and He will make your paths straight."
(Proverbs 3:4-6)

FRIDAY

 ## THE SPACE BETWEEN

Oftentimes, there is a gap between when God makes a promise and when that promise is fulfilled. Think about the story of Abraham and Sarah. God made a promise to Abraham (then Abram) when he was 75 years old – a promise that God would give him a son. This seems like an incredibly ridiculous promise. In fact, his wife, Sarah (then Sarai) heard this promise and broke out laughing! Now, if I were Abraham, I would think that God had better hurry up on His promise, because He was already about 50 years behind schedule, but after a year went by, Abraham still didn't have a son. It wasn't until he was 100 years old that this promised child, Isaac, was born!

Why would God wait so long to fulfill His promise? Why waste all those years of waiting? We often dismiss times of waiting as a waste of time. Standing in line at the grocery store, sitting at the DMV, or counting down the days to our next weekend or vacation can be painful. We wish we could just fast forward through, but what if these times of waiting are the times of our greatest growth?

God often uses these times of waiting in order to change us and draw us closer to Him. In the space between a promise given and a promise fulfilled lies a road to a deeper relationship with God.

WHEN I WAS CAUGHT IN THE IN-BETWEEN

In April of 2014, my mother passed away. My husband and I flew from our home in Washington State to Michigan, where we spent the week with family, making funeral preparations, and walking through the woods that surrounded my parents' house. Upon returning to Washington, I got what I thought was the flu. Weeks and weeks passed, and I did not begin to feel any better. Believing that it was just exhaustion from all the physical and emotional strain of the funeral, I decided to give it some more time. Eventually, I was finding it difficult to get through my day, and so I began what became a long and arduous journey of doctors and tests and therapies and drugs. Steadily, I began to find it increasingly difficult to get out of bed in the morning. I would be driving to work, and completely forget where I was or where I was going. I began falling asleep at the wheel and had to give up driving altogether. I was experiencing more and more pain in my muscles and joints, all the while, with no understanding of what was going on.

One day, as I was getting into the car for my husband to drive me to work, the upper part of my body moved toward the car while my legs began walking backward. I could not get my legs to go in the direction I wanted them to! The deterioration continued until the day came that I was not able to stand up in the morning at all. My legs would not work and my muscles would not hold me. An entire year had passed since I had walked in those woods at my parents' house, when I was finally tested for and diagnosed with Neurological Lyme disease. With the way the disease works, the longer the time between infection and diagnosis, the more severe the symptoms, the more difficult they are to treat, and the less likely remission will occur.

For the next 2 ½ years, my husband had to carry me to the bathroom, dress me, fix my meals, and on occasion, drive home from work to pick me up off of the floor when I fell out of bed and got stuck there. This was not an easy time for us, yet because of the way God can turn anything meant for our harm into something for our good, I wouldn't trade that season for anything.

I had been hugely blessed with a community of people who knew (Yada) what God is like and how to see things from His perspective. I had learned that the first response I needed to have when faced with a crisis is to worship and then to be still and listen. When I started to realize that this was not just exhaustion or a bout with the flu, I chose to step back and ask God, "What is going on here? What are You up to? This is starting to look pretty bad, and I know You. I know that what You have for me is greater than what is facing me. What is your promise for me in this?" And I just listened.

After about a week of just coming before Him and listening, I heard this whispered in my spirit: "When you are on the other side of this, you are going to be unrecognizable to yourself."

Okay. Here was my promise. Sometimes it may seem a little unclear. We like obvious, loud, booming answers, and yet God still speaks in a gentle whisper. This is what I realized as I meditated on this promise: 1) There was going to be an "other side" of this situation, meaning that God would eventually heal me, and 2) He was going to use this situation to transform me into His image in some pretty amazing ways. The best promises are not necessarily about how God is going to resolve our issue, but about who we get to become through the process.

This is where the abiding begins. I had some significant anxiety over the whole situation. I was able to work less and less, and eventually had to quit my job completely. It was our family's primary source of income! I felt physically miserable, in constant pain, and frequently nauseous. It hurt too much to sit up on most days, so I could do nothing but lie flat in bed. In fact, I was unable to do anything! If I could crawl to the bathroom on my own, it was a good day. I couldn't think clearly. I couldn't use my hands to at least write or make something. I could do NOTHING. I could only lie there and BE. This was very stressful at first! But I had my promise and my ability to abide in God. It took a number of weeks, but eventually a deep peace settled in my heart and grabbed hold of me. I realized that there was a deep level of anxiety about money and provision that had been a part of me my whole life, and God wanted to free me from that anxiety so that I could trust Him more.

As I lay in bed week after week, I could feel the anxiety leaving me, as an overwhelming peace and trust in God began to rise. I actually stopped praying for healing, because I knew God was going to heal me when He was ready, and I didn't want to miss out on any of the freedom and gifts He wanted to give me through this season. With the exception of my husband, everyone around me was distraught over my situation, but I had nothing but peace. I would be carried into the doctor's office with rigid, uncontrollable tremors, and the nurses would continually exclaim, "Why aren't you completely freaking out right now!"

This is the power of God in our lives, friends. This is what is intended to set us apart from the rest of the world and be **good** news to those who are lost and hurting. We were not sent to proclaim *okay* news, or *It's-what-I-have-to-do-to-go-to-Heaven* news, or *Eat-your-vegetables; they-are-good-for-you"* kind of good news, it is amazing, baffling, fantastic, *peace-in-the-midst-of-crisis,* *joy-in-the-midst-of-opposition*, *comfort-in-the-midst-of-grief* kind of GOOD NEWS!

Eventually, one night as I was resting in the peace of God before going to sleep, I heard Him whisper to me about how He brings wholeness, about His tenderness, and about how He is The Healer. I fell asleep to His whispers over my heart and feeling His gentleness cover me. When I awoke the next morning, I began the daily process of seeing if I would be able to crawl myself to the bathroom – a process which, if successful, would take about 45 minutes or so to get from lying in the bed to the bathroom across the hall. I started to roll over, brought my feet over the side of my bed – and stood up! Without any pain! I just stood there, dumbfounded and in shock, and then I walked to the bathroom like a normal person! Just like that! Just that quietly and peacefully, God declared that I was healed, and I was!

Here is the thing. That peace that I found never left me. That trust in Him continues to grow. It enabled me to say *yes* to God in circumstances where I otherwise might have let my anxiety have the last say. Because of this, my husband and I have followed God's leading, even when the rest of the world called us crazy or irresponsible. It brought us to places of being able to live in faith and live full of His Grace, Promise and Provision for us, and has made us living witnesses of His Kingdom in ways we would not have otherwise been able to be. We have been changed by Him in ways that never would have happened had I been healed instantly or had never gotten sick at all. Because He had taught me to hang on to His promises and to look for something better from Him, rather than beg for instant rescue, I not only got healed, but I also truly became unrecognizable to myself, and, once again, His promise to me was a *yes* in Christ.

 **BECOMING ROOTED**

Growing deep roots takes time. There can be a sort of pressure that roots experience as they expand and inhabit more space in the soil. We can also experience a sort of pressure as we grow deeper in God. Our greatest transformations result from walking with God through our most difficult times. If you are struggling, take hope, God's promise for you is so much greater than your difficulty.

"For we know that our present sufferings are not worth comparing
with the glory that will be revealed in us."
(Romans 8:18)

 **PRAYER**

God, it can be so hard to face life's circumstances day after day, with no apparent relief. Come close to me in those places. Hold me tightly. Whisper Your promises to my heart until I am changed into Your image. I choose to trust Your love and Your goodness, even when it is hard to see. Let this be the place where my heart meets with Yours, and You cover me with Your love. Let this struggle be the beginning of my powerful testimony of Who You are.

Amen.

REACHING DEEPER

Tomorrow, we will take a closer look at how to take the promises God has for us and dig deeper into all that God wants to do in and through us in our circumstances.

WEEK THREE

DEEPLY ROOTED IN THE PROMISES OF GOD

WHEN WE FIND OURSELVES STANDING ON AN UNSHAKABLE FOUNDATION

SATURDAY

 AN EXERCISE IN GOING DEEPER

As in my example, sometimes the resolution we are most desperately hoping for takes a long time to come. In fact, it may be that the resolution we receive isn't necessarily what we originally wanted. What we can be sure of, though, is that no matter what we are going through, God has a promise for us that outshines our present suffering.

"For we know that our present sufferings are not worth comparing with the glory that will be revealed in us."
(Romans 8:18)

Our faith in Christ is not about having a genie in a bottle that we can call on to give us our wishes when times get difficult. It is about having a loving Lord who promises to be with us every step of the way. It is about learning how to travel the space between a promise given and a promise received with a Guide (the Holy Spirit) who wants to make sure that we don't miss any good gifts that God wants to give us on the way.

Christianity, if I may say it again, is primarily about cultivating a relationship with Christ. It is the long, difficult seasons – viewed from God's perspective – that bring about the greatest transformation in us. The promises that God gives us are so much more than an instant answer to prayer. They are stepping stones to a deeper understanding of who God is and what He is like. They are the relationship-builders of a life spent with the Life Giver.

Today we are going to learn how to travel that space between a promise given and a promise received in such a way that we not only receive our promise, but we don't miss any of God's good and perfect gifts He has placed along the way.

 # QUESTIONS/ACTIVITIES

1. Take out your promise that you wrote on Thursday and rewrite it here.

_____

_____

_____

_____

2. Elaborate on what that promise means to your situation.

_____

_____

_____

_____

3. Thank God for this promise.

4. Ask God how you can align with this promise. Is there a step of faith He is asking you to take? Write it here.

_____

_____

_____

_____

_____

5. Is there a fruit of the Spirit that you can grow in through this
    situation? Write it here.

_____

_____

_____

_____

_____

6. Ask God to show you what that fruit of the Spirit looks like in
    the life of Christ.

_____

_____

_____

_____

_____

_____

7. Ask God how He is calling you to become more like Christ through this circumstance.

_____

_____

_____

_____

_____

8. Ask God to show you what you will look like at the end of this situation as you and the Holy Spirit intentionally seek to use it to become more like Christ.

_____

_____

_____

_____

_____

This is the real prize at the end of this process. It is God at work in us, making us more like Christ. As we seek Him first – and His Kingdom – all the other stuff falls into place. It is another one of those amazing promises that Jesus made us. (Matt. 6:33).

 BECOMING DEEPLY ROOTED

Through this process, we are looking for something far more powerful than a quick rescue. We are looking for a Heavenly Kingdom to break into our lives and into the lives of those around us. Through this process, we are looking to be changed into the image of Christ.

 PRAYER

God, thank You so much for leading me to the promises You have given me for just this circumstance. Thank You that You are faithful, not only to keep Your promises, but also to draw me closer to Your heart and to make me more like You in the waiting. Help me keep my eyes on You instead of on what is going on around me, and may Your Kingdom break through into my life in a way that transforms me into a powerful witness of Who You are and what You are like. Thank You that You are always so good to me.

Amen.

WEEK FOUR

DEEPLY ROOTED IN THE PRESENCE OF GOD

WHEN WE EXPERIENCE THE RELATIONSHIP WITH GOD WE WERE MEANT TO HAVE

WEEK FOUR

DEEPLY ROOTED IN THE PRESENCE OF GOD

WHEN WE EXPERIENCE THE RELATIONSHIP WITH GOD WE WERE MEANT TO HAVE

> *"This is where I'm meant to be.*
> *Me in you and you in me.*
> *I don't have to prove a thing.*
> *You've already approved of me."*
> *"Communion" by Maverick City Music*

"I am the vine; you are the branches.
If you remain in me and I in you, you will bear much fruit;
apart from me you can do nothing."
(John 15:5)

MONDAY

 ## STAYING PLUGGED INTO THE SOURCE

Confession time: I am kind of a lazy housekeeper. I like things relatively picked up and wiped down, but window washing and deep corner dusting do not occur very often at my house. When it comes to vacuuming, I like to find the plug that will let me cover the greatest amount of carpet area, and I use the full length of that cord. I cannot tell you how many times in one round of vacuuming that I go too far and the vacuum shuts off as the plug pulls out of the socket. Unfortunately, the way a vacuum is built, it needs to stay near and plugged into its source of power in order to work. When it is not plugged in, it is nothing more than a lint holder.

This is much like our Christian lives. We cannot do anything on our own. We must remain near and connected to our Source of power, our Source of strength, our Source of life. This goes radically against our western mindsets. We have become a culture that prides itself in our independence. We are the *pull-yourself-up-by-your-own-bootstraps*, *get-er-done*, and *just do it* culture. This mindset has also slipped into our Christian language. How many of you have heard or been told, "God helps those who help themselves"? How about, "God will never give you more than you can handle"? The problem is that these sayings are not biblical. We were never created to help ourselves, nor were we created to handle everything that comes our way. We were not designed for independence. In fact, we were designed for radical dependency – on God.

As soon as we put our trust in Him, we find ourselves positioned IN Him, and He is positioned IN us. We are surrounded on the inside and out! Yet, it is so easy to slip back into relying on our own strength to get us through. This happens so quickly and so subtly. We find ourselves looking at our finances and trying to make a plan to make ends meet. We keep adding things to our "to do" list and decide that we just have to stay at work a little longer, move a little faster, or multitask a little more efficiently in order to get things done. Our circumstances feel far more tangible to us than the presence of God that surrounds us, and before we know it, God becomes an add-on to our task list. "After I fix dinner and get the kids ready, I will take a few moments of devotional time." We make our financial plans and ask God to bless our efforts. We do all that we can, and then hope that God will take it from there.

What if God wants to be the creator of that financial plan? What if He wants to bring peace and joy to bedtime with the kids? He wants to lead from the beginning, not just step in when we have run out of options and energy. In order to let Him run things, we need to learn how to remain close and plugged into Him – not just during our morning or evening prayer time, not just as a recharge on Sundays, and not just when we find ourselves in crisis mode – but throughout every day. This is the place where true change can occur in our lives. This is the place where we exchange our anxiety and exhaustion for God's rest and peace. It's where we exchange our weakness for God's power, and we exchange our attempts to get by for God's abundance and fullness.

BECOMING ROOTED

One of my favorite images from scripture is the one from John 15:5:

> *"I am the vine; you are the branches.*
> *If you remain in me and I in you,*
> *you will bear much fruit;*
> *apart from me you can do nothing."*

This is a beautiful picture of the oneness we were created to have with Christ, much like the oneness that Jesus always had with the Father. He says that He does nothing on His own, but only speaks what the Father is speaking and does what the Father is doing. (John 5:30). What perfect unity – and this same gift of unity is now available to us through the Holy Spirit. Christ has done this work for us on the cross. Our job is just to remain.

PRAYER

God, I confess that I can't do it all on my own. I am sorry for the times that I try to figure out life without You. Thank You that You have all the wisdom, strength, and rest that I need. Show me how to draw near to You – and how to stay there.

Amen.

REACHING DEEPER

So how do we remain in Christ? What does that mean? Tomorrow we are going to take a look at what this looks like in our hectic, day-to-day lives, and learn some simple and practical tips for remaining in Christ.

WEEK FOUR

DEEPLY ROOTED IN THE PRESENCE OF GOD

WHEN WE EXPERIENCE THE RELATIONSHIP WITH GOD WE WERE MEANT TO HAVE

TUESDAY

 ## AN EXERCISE IN GOING DEEPER

How often during our week are we aware that God is with us? So often we go through our entire day, through all of our small and large obstacles, without realizing that there is someone right there Who is just waiting to take all our stresses and give us His peace. He is there, holding the wisdom and guidance we need, while we try to figure out how to make decisions. He is there when we are feeling tired. He is there when our kid just made their first soccer goal. He is there when we are facing a sink full of dishes after a long day.

Too often, we reserve our awareness of God's presence for Sunday mornings and earth-shattering crises. Imagine all of the grace and peace and joy we are missing! When that time of crisis comes, we have not learned how to receive from Him, and we are left overwhelmed by our circumstances.

The beautiful thing is that it does not take a lot of hard work to practice being aware that He is with us. It does not require hours of Bible study or going through long lists of prayer requests. It's simply an invitation to acknowledge that God is with us throughout the day. When the pressures of the day begin to build, we get to step back into His presence, take a deep breath, and say "Thank You, God, that You are right here with me, inviting me to rest in Your arms of power and peace." When something unexpectedly good happens, we get to take a moment to praise Him, "God, you are so awesome! Thank you!" When we are scrubbing the dishes, we can turn to Him and chat with Him about whatever is on our minds. I know someone who gets up in the morning and makes tea for himself – and God. It is a tangible reminder for him that he will not be going through the day alone. He sits at the table and just starts his day off with a chat with God about what his day looks like, and he takes some time to listen to God's perspective on what his day is *actually* going to be about.

Today we are going to go through a simple exercise to determine our starting point, our "You are here sticker" on the map, and use that spot to grow and expand in our awareness of God's presence in our lives.

QUESTIONS/ACTIVITIES

1. Find a quiet place where you can be still *(rapha - let go)* and know *(yada - touch)* that He is God.

2. Ask God to help you become more sensitive to His presence and His voice.

3. Think about a time when you felt connected to God. Perhaps it was a sense of His love during a time of prayer. Maybe you felt awed by His Glory during a time of worship. Maybe you felt a sense of peace and majesty while you were out in nature. Write your thoughts here about where you were, what you were doing, and what you felt or sensed about God.

_____

_____

_____

_____

_____

4. God made us all beautifully unique so that we could all be part of an expression of Who He is. Since we are all wired differently, we may find unique ways in which we connect to God most easily. Some of us may feel most connected while we are

meditating on His Word. Some of us may feel most connected to God while interacting with others. Some of us may find ourselves talking with God most easily while we are driving or walking. Take a look at what you wrote above, and think about what kind of activities you feel most connected to God while doing. Write them here.

_____

_____

_____

_____

_____

5. This is your starting point. It is your own personal entryway into God's presence. While we are always positioned in Christ, it takes spiritual muscles to increase our *awareness* of His presence. Much like our physical muscles, our spiritual muscles require exercise in order to strengthen. Imagine if you were training for a marathon, but decided you were going to run only on Sunday mornings! You wouldn't get very far. However, if you decided to start with a brisk five-minute walk for the first week and slowly increase that each week, you would find yourself getting stronger and jogging farther without burnout or injury.

6. Rewrite your answer to Question #4. Set aside five minutes a day to connect with God in this way.

7. Each day this week, come back to this space and write down what you experienced. What did you find yourself praying about? Did you sense peace or joy? What did God show you about yourself or your circumstances? What did God show you about Himself? Did a scripture come to mind? If you didn't notice anything, that's fine. Write that here as well. Sometimes when we feel Him the least, He is doing the most in us, so don't let that discourage you. Just thank Him for surrounding you with His love, no matter what your experience is.

 **BECOMING DEEPLY ROOTED**

A tree continues to gain nourishment from being in the soil every day. As you practice being in God's presence on a daily basis, you will find yourself being filled with more of God's peace, joy, and strength than you ever thought possible!

 **PRAYER**

Ever-present God, thank You that You are nearer to me than I can even comprehend. Open my eyes and my heart to see You and connect with You every day and in every situation. Open my ears to hear Your voice, and continue to draw me into conversations with You, so that I may be drawn deeper into relationship with You.

Amen.

*If you are interested in learning more about this process, I suggest reading the great Christian classic, **The Practice of the Presence of God** by Brother Lawrence.*

WEEK FOUR

DEEPLY ROOTED IN THE PRESENCE OF GOD

WHEN WE EXPERIENCE THE RELATIONSHIP WITH GOD WE WERE MEANT TO HAVE

> *"This is where I'm meant to be.*
> *Me in you..."*
> *"Communion" by Maverick City Music*

*Acts 17:28 "For **in** Him we live*
and move and have our being."

WEDNESDAY

 ## YOU ARE POSITIONED IN CHRIST

There is an even greater promise that we get to explore than the truth that God is always with us. Even closer than sitting next to us at the table or standing next to us while we do the dishes, because of Jesus, we are positioned **in** Christ! (And since Jesus and the Father are one, we are **in** God!)

Psalm 91 is a great description of what this looks like when we face trials.

> *"Whoever **dwells in** the shelter of the Most High will **rest in** the shadow of the Almighty (vs. 1)...He will cover you with His feathers, and under His wings you will find refuge (vs. 4)... If you say 'The LORD is my refuge', and you make the Most High your dwelling, no harm will overtake you, no disaster will come near your tent. (vs. 9-10)"*

David understood that when everything comes against us, it is **in** God that we are covered and shielded. When God is our Dwelling Place, where we abide and remain, we find rest and refuge and safety.

In the Old Testament, the presence of God could only be found in the temple or the tabernacle, and only a rare few would be allowed to enter. Only a handful of people – over hundreds of years – were ever able to be **in** the presence of God!

THE ONE THAT REMAINED

There is an interesting passage in Exodus 33:7-11 that describes what this was like for the Israelites as they were wandering through the desert. It explains that Moses had a tent that he called "the Tent of Meeting." If anyone had something they wanted to bring before God, they would go and wait outside of this tent, as Moses would go inside. When Moses went inside the tent, a pillar of cloud would cover the entrance while God talked to Moses. In fact, scripture so beautifully says, "The Lord would speak to Moses face to face, as one speaks to a friend." And listen to the rest of verse 11: "Then Moses would return to the camp, *but his young aid Joshua, son of Nun, would not leave the tent.*"

This is someone who understood the power of abiding in the presence of God! He understood John 15:5 long before it was ever written. While Moses had this beautiful face-to-face talk with God, and then would go back to business as usual, Joshua knew that apart from God's presence, he could do nothing. Joshua REFUSED to leave. A branch attached to a vine digs in. It becomes engrafted until there is no separation. Is it any wonder that it was Joshua, and not Moses, who ended up leading Israel into the Promised Land? We can't accomplish anything for God on our own, yet in God, we can accomplish all things! Our invitation is not to just pop our head into a church building on a Sunday morning. It is to chase after and dig into the presence of God, to dwell there, to remain there, and to, like Joshua, refuse to leave! And why would we want to do anything else? For "In His presence is fullness of joy!" (Psalms 16:11)

 **BECOMING ROOTED**

Thanks to Christ and His gift of The Holy Spirit, we no longer need to rely on a tent of meeting in order to be in God's presence. We are now positioned in Christ every moment of every day! Our job, like the branch to the vine, is to remain.

 **PRAYER**

God, what an AMAZING TRUTH it is that I am always in You! You keep me with You, no matter how I am feeling or behaving. Remind me throughout my day that You are surrounding me, and draw me into conversation with You. I choose to rely on You and rest in You, no matter what circumstances come up for me in my day, knowing that You are the One Who will get me through – knowing that it's You Who brings me joy!

Amen.

 **REACHING DEEPER**

Tomorrow we will continue to practice remaining in God's presence. We will continue to build our "God awareness" muscles until we instinctively acknowledge His presence with us and learn to keep our spiritual ears open to His voice throughout every part of our day. This is how we learn what it means to "pray without ceasing."

"Rejoice always, pray continually, give thanks in all circumstances; for this is God's will for you in Christ Jesus."
(1 Thessalonians 5:16-18)

WEEK FOUR

DEEPLY ROOTED IN THE PRESENCE OF GOD

WHEN WE EXPERIENCE THE RELATIONSHIP WITH GOD WE WERE MEANT TO HAVE

THURSDAY

 ## AN EXERCISE IN GOING DEEPER

Yesterday we learned about the beautiful gift we have of being positioned in Christ. We looked at the heart of Joshua as he refused to leave the presence of God. Thankfully, we no longer have to rely on being inside of a tent in order to be in God's presence. We have already been placed in Christ, and we are in His presence every moment of every day.

The difficulty with remaining in God's presence, though, is that our hectic and busy lives constantly scream for our attention. *Sure,* you think, *It must be nice if you are a cloistered hermit that lives alone in the woods, but I have four kids and a full time job! How am I supposed to remain in God's presence all day long?*

First of all, God loves to lavish His grace on you. This is not another thing to add to your already overflowing to-do list. God wants to connect with you throughout your day so that you can be filled with His peace when the kids are throwing a tantrum. He wants to give you wisdom and direction when you're facing difficult decisions, and He wants to empower you with His grace when you are up against impossible deadlines.

Doesn't that sound like Good News? Below, we will walk through a simple exercise that will help you begin to easily and naturally build in small moments with the Lord throughout your day that will result in huge blessings in your mind, emotions, and life.

 # QUESTIONS/ACTIVITES

1. Find a quiet place where you can be still *(rapha - let go)* and know *(yada - touch)* that He is God.

2. Set aside five to ten minutes each day this week to just sit quietly with God and be with Him. Write about your experience here.

_____

_____

_____

3. Take some time this week to go for a nature walk or take a relaxing drive with God. Talk to Him about what you see and experience. Thank Him for the beauty of creation. Enjoy your time alone with Him. Enjoy Him. Write about your experience here.

_____

_____

_____

_____

_____

4. Begin to practice remaining in God throughout your day. All this means is that as you go throughout your day, take a moment every so often to acknowledge that God is with you. Thank Him that He is going through this day with you. Quiet yourself (ra-pha - let go) for a moment and listen for His voice. See if God has any direction or encouragement for you in this part of your day. Write down your experiences or anything He shows you.

    Tip: it might be helpful to stop and take a couple of deep breaths as you do this. This physical act will often help to quiet your mind *and calm your emotions in the middle of a hectic day, making it easier to become still before God and listen for His gentle whisper.*

_____

_____

_____

_____

_____

5. If helpful, build in some tangible reminders to yourself to practice God's presence throughout the day, such as sending yourself notifications, placing a sticky note at your desk, or making this practice a part of a daily routine such as washing the dishes.

 **BECOMING DEEPLY ROOTED**

As you continue to build this simple practice into your day, you will find yourself not just acknowledging His nearness, but having great conversations with God. You will be amazed at how much more God has in store for your everyday life than you ever imagined! As you practice, continue to take note of how it went. Did you notice a difference in your level of peace throughout the week? Did God show you something about your job or a situation that gave you a different perspective? Be sure to write down your experiences.

 **PRAYER**

Jesus, thank You that You are always here, ready and waiting for me to turn my face and my attention toward You. Help me experience Your presence and grow more in love with You. Create in me and in my life, the space I need to connect with You and to hear from You.

Amen.

WEEK FOUR

DEEPLY ROOTED IN THE PRESENCE OF GOD

WHEN WE EXPERIENCE THE RELATIONSHIP WITH GOD WE WERE MEANT TO HAVE

"This is where I'm meant to be.
...you in me"
"Communion" by Maverick City Music

"To them God has chosen to make
known among the Gentiles the glorious riches of this mystery,
*which is Christ **in you**, the hope of glory."*
(Colossians 1:27)

FRIDAY

 ## GOD DWELLS IN YOU

Not only have we been permanently positioned in God's presence, but God's presence lives in us. We are surrounded! In Christ, we find refuge and safety. The Holy Spirit living in us transforms us, empowers us, and makes us more like Christ.

I had a funny situation one day when I distinctly recognized Christ in me being at odds with me. I suspect this happens a lot more often than I would like to admit. However, on this occasion, what I was thinking and feeling was overwritten by Christ in me, and thankfully I was aware enough of what was going on to just let Him take over.

 ## CHRIST IN ME VS ME

For most of my childhood and through much of my college years, I mowed lawns for a living. In those days, it was not common for a girl to be running her own lawn mowing business, and I had a couple of clients that were determined to make it more difficult for me. One man in particular refused to have any dealings with me personally. He would make out the check to my father and send it to him in the mail. He would often come outside and just glare at me as I mowed. One day, as I was moving from the back yard to the front yard, he came storming out at me and screaming. I turned my mower off and turned to face him. He was in my face, screaming that as I was going from the back yard to the front yard he had let his dog out, and his dog got out through the fence and ran away.

I stood there as thoughts of my own began running through my head. When I opened my mouth, however, this humble, sincere, kind voice came out of me saying "I am so sorry. That is just awful. Is there anything I can do?" Now, that was NOT what was going on in my thoughts, mind you. My thoughts were more like, *Jerk! You were the one who let your dog out while your lawn was being mowed. What did you think would happen?* I was stunned by not just the words, but the *spirit* that came out of me in that moment. This began a hilarious three-way conversation between this man, the Holy Spirit (taking over my words and actions), and me that resulted in a little miracle.

The Holy Spirit flowing through me: "I am so sorry. That is just awful. If there anything I can do?

My thought: Where did that come from? That sounded REALLY nice, and NOT what I am thinking or feeling!

Man: (still screaming) "You have no idea what you have done! The last time he ran away, I had to chase him for several hours through the neighborhood before I caught him! I will never get him back!"

My thought: Can you blame him?

The Holy Spirit speaking out loud through me: "Again, I am deeply sorry (full-on genuine concern and gentle kindness). May I help you look for him?"

My thought: *What am I going to do that this guy can't? Plus, I still have a ton of lawns to mow today.*

Man: (still screaming) "What are you going to do that I can't!"

The Holy Spirit speaking out through me: (thick with kindness and gentleness) "Would it be okay if I at least tried?"

My thought: *Okay. I know the Holy Spirit is doing this, so I am just going to go with it.*

Man: (screaming). "Whatever. It's not going to do you any good! You've ruined my whole day, and I may never get my dog back!"

Me: I found myself slowly turning away from him and kneeling down in the grass, facing the road.

Me: ???????!!!!!!!

Man: (He was stunned into silence and I could feel him staring, jaw agape, at this crazy woman's back.)

Me: I just knelt there stunned myself. *What was I doing? How long was I going to kneel here? And how am I going to make a casual and graceful transition from kneeling on the ground to going back to mowing his lawn?*

After about five seconds of kneeling on the grass, I could see a small bundle of white fluff bolting around a corner about half a mile down the road. My eyes wide, I watched this little thing just run as fast as his legs could carry him down the sidewalk, across the street, across the lawn, and jump straight into my arms! I sat there and blinked a few times.

My thought: Be cool. Be cool.

I slowly stood up, turned around, and handed the dog back to the man.

As I turned to face the man, my heart was melted by the love of the Holy Spirit within me. I gave the man a genuine, kind smile as I said, "Here you go," and handed him his dog.

He kept staring at my shirt, and then, at me. He just mumbled over and over, "I don't believe it. I don't believe it." He managed a "Thank you," before he turned around and walked into his house with his dog.

After he was gone, I remembered that he was staring at my shirt, and I looked down to see what he was looking at. That morning, I had thrown on an old shirt I got while on a mission trip with YWAM (Youth with a Mission). The shirt said "If you want to see the things of God, you must walk like Jesus did."

After that day, that man came out to greet me every time I mowed his lawn, and he always had a huge smile on his face. He paid me double. He sent me a Christmas card with cash in it every year. He was like Scrooge on Christmas Morning!

I had begun that day just going about my business and finding myself face-to-face with an irate customer. Christ in me, on the other hand, had arranged an unexpected encounter with His Glory for both this man and me.

BECOMING ROOTED

A healthy tree becomes very adept at taking water and nutrients up through its roots, up through its trunk, and out through its branches where fruit can grow. As we continue to spend more time rooted in the presence of God, we become more sensitive to His voice and His heart in us. When our voice begins to speak the words of Christ, and our hearts begin to love with the heart of Christ, we are transformed into His image.

# PRAYER

Dear Jesus, what an unspeakable gift You have given me in the person of the Holy Spirit! You made it so that I would never be alone. I never have to try to please You from my own strength. You live in me, so that through me, You can bring glory to Yourself. Help me become more sensitive to Your Spirit. Help me hear You speaking, so that I can speak Your words. Help me feel Your love so that I can love others in the same way. Help me see You at work so that I can come alongside You. Father, I want to be like Jesus, only saying what I hear You say and only doing what I see You do. (John 5:19). Thank You for Your desire and Your faithfulness to make me more like Christ.

Amen.

REACHING DEEPER

In this story, God used me to bless the heart of someone else with the fruit of His Spirit. Tomorrow we will learn how to connect with God's presence in us so that we may be able to intentionally cultivate the fruit of His Spirit in our lives.

"I am the vine; you are the branches.
If you remain in me and I in you, you will bear much fruit;
apart from me you can do nothing."
(John 15:5)

WEEK FOUR

DEEPLY ROOTED IN THE PRESENCE OF GOD

WHEN WE EXPERIENCE THE RELATIONSHIP WITH GOD WE WERE MEANT TO HAVE

SATURDAY

 ## AN EXERCISE IN GOING DEEPER

This story of the escaped dog remains to this day, one of my most treasured encounters with God. I have seen countless healings, deliverances, and miracles of God. I have seen 80,000 people come to Christ in one night. But this occasion was different. There was no conference. I wasn't on a mission trip. There was no loud or gigantic move of God. There was an angry man, a little dog, and me on a VERY day-like-every-other-day, kind of day.

There was not even any great miracle. He didn't get healed (not physically anyway). I didn't have some great word from the Lord to share with him. It was simply the Holy Spirit living inside me, pouring out His fruit of love, joy, peace, patience, kindness, and self-control to a man who desperately needed it. He used me in spite of myself, in order to touch someone with His kindness.

No matter who you are, if you are a Christian, you have the Holy Spirit living inside you. Our great joy is to not only experience the gifts of the Holy Spirit, but also His fruit. Oftentimes, the expression of the fruit of the Spirit – a smile of kindness, a warm hug, or sitting quietly next to someone who is hurting – can change the course of someone's day – or even the course of their life!

Like any fruit-bearing plant, however, we have the opportunity to tend, cultivate and nourish the fruit of the Spirit that we bear. Let's look at John 15:5 one more time:

> *"I am the vine; you are the branches.*
> *If you remain in me and I in you, you will bear much fruit;*
> *apart from me you can do nothing."*

We can work really hard at trying to be patient, loving, or kind, but have you ever noticed how easily – in the heat of the moment – frustration, bitterness, anxiety, or discouragement can rise up within us? In my story yesterday, what was rising up within me was NOT in line with the fruit of the spirit! Thankfully, in that situation, the Holy Spirit decided to shove me aside and take over. What God desires, however, is that we *join* Him in what He is doing! The secret to becoming a person that overflows with the fruit of the Spirit in those moments is not trying to will ourselves to be better people. It is our abiding and remaining in God that produces much fruit!

Today we will go through a short exercise in learning how to intentionally join with what God wants to do in us in order to make us more like Christ.

 # QUESTIONS/ACTIVITIES

1. Find a quiet place where you can be still *(rapha - let go)* and know *(yada - touch)* that He is God.

2. Ask God to help you to become sensitive to His voice and His presence.

3. Ask God to show you how He is currently at work making you more like Christ. Write down what He shows you here.

_____

_____

_____

_____

_____

4. Take a moment and consider the fruit of the Spirit: love, joy peace, patience, kindness, goodness, faithfulness, gentleness, and self-control. Is there one of these fruits that you wish you had more of in your life? Write that fruit here and put it in the blanks in the prayer below.

5. Now we have the invitation to abide in Christ. What does that fruit look like in the life of Christ? Is there a story from the Gospels where He demonstrated that fruit? Write that here.

_____

_____

_____

_____

_____

6. Is there a scripture that comes to mind about that particular fruit of the Spirit? Write that here.

_____

_____

_____

_____

_____

7. Ask God to show you what you would look like, act like, and feel like if you were filled to overflowing with that fruit of the Spirit. Write down what He shows you.

As an example, a fruit I would like to experience more of is joy. In asking the Lord to show me more about His joy, I imagine Jesus playing with the children and laughing. The Holy Spirit reminds me of the verse, "The joy of the Lord is my strength." These things are an invitation from the Lord for me to dwell in His joy.

BECOMING DEEPLY ROOTED

We don't become more like Christ by trying harder to behave better. We become more like Christ by dwelling and remaining in Christ. The more deeply we are rooted in the presence of God, the more we are able to receive from Him the fruit of His Spirit. II Cor. 3:18 says, *"And we all, who with unveiled faces behold (or contemplate) the Lord's glory, are being transformed into*

His image with ever-increasing glory, which comes from the Lord, who is the Spirit."

As we think about (contemplate) and turn our hearts to look on (behold) Who God is, we become more like Him! As we behold His joy, we are changed by His joy into joyful people!

 # PRAYER

Lord, please show me what Your __(fruit of the Spirit)__ is like. Open my eyes to see the __(fruit of the Spirit)__ on Your face and to feel the __(fruit of the Spirit)__ in Your heart. Transform me into Your image as You reveal more of Yourself to me and fill me with Your __(fruit of the Spirit)__.

Amen.

WEEK FIVE

DEEPLY ROOTED IN THE IMAGE OF GOD

WHEN WE DISCOVER OUR UNIQUE AND POWERFUL IDENTITY IN CHRIST

WEEK FIVE

DEEPLY ROOTED IN THE IMAGE OF GOD

WHEN WE DISCOVER OUR UNIQUE AND POWERFUL IDENTITY IN CHRIST

"I want you to live in confidence that when God looks at you He sees beauty.
He sees value. He sees hope."
Tammy Maltby

"But this is what the LORD says - He who created you,
He who formed you, 'Do not fear, for I have redeemed you;
I have called you by name and you are mine.'"
(Isaiah 43:1)

MONDAY

 ## A BETTER NAME

From the time we were very little, most, if not all of us, discovered the destructive power of name-calling. "Stupid, Geek, Ugly, Fat, Chicken, Loser, and the list goes on.

The problem is, they often seem to live on in us through adulthood. They somehow find their way into our own self-definitions. They rise up to the forefront of our thoughts when we find ourselves facing our own insecurities.

What names and thoughts arise in you, especially when you try to grow and step out of your comfort zone? I can tell you that even as I write this book, I am faced with the shy and timid girl who wouldn't speak, because she decided it was safer to become invisible.

"People aren't going to get this."

"They are going to think it's stupid."

"You don't have anything meaningful to say."

"You might as well give up."

"It's not going to be any good."

These negative thoughts are daunting and often leave us huddled in our safe places, unwilling or unable to try new things or grow. The challenge to this, though, especially as we learn to listen to God's voice and obey His direction, is that He RARELY, if ever, asks us to do something we are completely comfortable with. The fact is, the more we grow in Him, the further outside our comfort zones He takes us.

The GOOD NEWS is that there is a joyful and empowering answer to this challenge. The answer lies in the fact that He sees us much differently than the way others see us or even the way we see ourselves, and because He is the One Who created us, we can trust His perspective above anyone else's.

Scripture is filled with names that He calls us, His children. It doesn't matter what our personality is like, what happened in our past, what other people have said about us, or what we have said about ourselves. What God says about us is what is true. He is the One Who created us. Scripture says that even before the world was created, He knew exactly who we were going to be – and it was *good*. He sees us fully redeemed through the eyes of Christ and the power of the cross, and He calls us by THAT name. We can joyfully leave behind all the other names that we have been called, as well as the names we call ourselves, and embrace His name for us.

 THE TURTLE VS THE LIONESS

I have always been a very quiet, socially awkward person. In fact, I have often felt this symbiotic relationship with turtles...spending most of my time with my head and arms hiding within a shell, only occasionally popping my neck out to see what is going on around me. If you were to put me at a party, you would most likely find me sitting in a corner with a death grip on my chair or taking frequent walks to the bathroom or outside in order to breathe. Growing up, I was so quiet that even in the moments that I felt relatively comfortable in a group situation, inevitably someone would look at me and say, "You sure don't talk much, do you?" It is an identity that I have never really been able to get away from.

God has a different name for me, though. You see, deep down, I have always known that this is the area of my greatest redemption.

God often uses the area of our greatest weakness as the point of our most powerful purpose. After all, he uses the weak things of the world to shame the strong. I know that because of my well-demonstrated weakness, God can receive much-deserved glory through me. God calls me by a different name. In the moments of my greatest shyness and timidity, He grins at me with a knowing twinkle in His eye and calls me His roaring lioness. I hear Him chuckle with the laugh of someone who is keeping a really great secret, and my face of anxiety transforms to match His grin. The two of us know something that the rest of the world can't yet see... who God made me to be.

 ## BECOMING ROOTED

If you are like me, you can't determine what a tree or flower is going to look like just from looking at a seed. It takes an expert to be able to decipher the name of the seed, the type of soil it requires, and the amount of sun and water it needs to grow into all that it is meant to be. Yet God knew us long before He created us, and He knew all that He meant for us to be. His voice is the only voice we need to listen to. The name that He calls us is our only true name.

 ## PRAYER

Loving Father, You know every hair on my head. You know every thought I have and everything I do when no one else is looking. You have seen me at my weakest and my worst, and yet You see me through the life of Your Son, Jesus. You see me whole, redeemed, free, bold and powerful, and You delight in every part of me. Help me trust Your perception of me. Help me see myself the way You do, and give me courage to live out the vision You have of my life.

Amen.

 # REACHING DEEPER

Tomorrow we will take a look at some of the many names that God calls us. We will go through a simple exercise in learning how to dwell in the truth of who we are in God.

WEEK FIVE

DEEPLY ROOTED IN THE IMAGE OF GOD

WHEN WE DISCOVER OUR UNIQUE AND POWERFUL IDENTITY IN CHRIST

TUESDAY

 ## AN EXERCISE IN GOING DEEPER

Yesterday we discovered that God sees us much differently than we see ourselves. We also learned that no matter what we think about ourselves, or what others think of us, only what God thinks of us matters. Only what God thinks about us is true.

So what *does* God think about us? Today we will be starting in the same place we have each week. We will be finding the "You are here" sticker on our trail map by taking a look at some of the many names that God declares over us in His Word.

QUESTIONS/ACTIVITIES

1. In the back of this book, I have created a list of some of the many things that God says about us in scripture. Turn to Appendix #Three, and take some time to look them over. Slowly read through them, and consider the truth in them. Again, I highly recommend that you read this list out loud. Something powerful happens when we declare these truths over ourselves.

2. Choose one identity statement from this list that stands out to you, and write it here.

_____

_____

_____

_____

_____

3. Ask God to show you what this statement means for your life. Write down what He shows you.

_____

_____

_____

_____

_____

4. Rewrite that statement somewhere you will see it throughout your day. Continue to declare this statement over yourself
   through the day, thanking God for this truth. Write down your
   experience here.

_____

_____

_____

_____

_____

 **BECOMING DEEPLY ROOTED**

Like my face of fear changing to a grin, something powerful
shifts inside of us as we learn to agree with what God says about
us instead of what anyone else thinks. Under God's smile of ap-
proval, we stand taller, become stronger, and shine brighter in a
dark world. The more we listen to God's heart for us, the more we
are changed into the person He sees when He looks at us.

 **PRAYER**

Father God, thank You that this is just a small taste of all the things You declare about me. It seems too good to be true, yet You are the TRUTH. Help me understand what these things mean for me and for my life. Show me how to receive these truths into my heart and my mind, so that I may be changed by the power of Your Word and Your Goodness.

Amen.

WEEK FIVE

DEEPLY ROOTED IN THE IMAGE OF GOD

WHEN WE DISCOVER OUR UNIQUE AND POWERFUL IDENTITY IN CHRIST

> *"I am no longer bound to the restraints of the person I used to be. In Christ, I have been made new, and because of that, I am free to never be the same again."*
> *Morgan Harper Nichols*

> *"Therefore if anyone is in Christ, he is a new creation. The old has gone, the new has come."*
> *(2 Corinthians 5:17)*

WEDNESDAY

 A NEW CREATION

So many of us have been raised to think of ourselves as lowly sinners who are incapable of anything good, and without God, this is true. However, when we first put our faith in God, we were changed forever at the very core. Our life now lies in Christ, and we are a NEW CREATION!

Consider the caterpillar. At its core, a caterpillar is a fuzzy, crawling insect. It inches along in life, rarely going more than ten meters from the place it was hatched. Then something miraculous happens. The caterpillar goes through an amazing transformation and becomes a beautiful butterfly. It isn't a caterpillar that evolved to learn some new skills; it is a completely new creation! As a caterpillar, it struggled to crawl a few meters, but as a butterfly, it can travel over three thousand miles in a season and can soar three quarters of a mile above the earth!

> *"A butterfly is never called 'a caterpillar saved by grace.'*
> *It's a completely new creation.*
> *The butterfly has left the cocoon behind."*
> *Lisa Thompson*

Like the caterpillar transforming into a butterfly, when we give our lives to Christ, we become something completely different and amazing! We were once broken and lost sinners, and then something miraculous happened to us – we were placed in Christ, and Christ came to live inside of us as the person of the Holy

Spirit! The apostle Paul sums up this transformation beautifully in Galatians 2:20:

> *"I have been crucified with Christ and I no longer live, but Christ lives in me. The life I now live in the body, I live by faith in the Son of God, who loved me and gave Himself for me."*

MY NEW IDENTITY

I have always enjoyed running. There is something very meditative and grounding in it for me as I listen to the steady pace of my feet touching the pavement and the rhythm of my breath. I ran track and cross country in High School and continued to enjoy the occasional run for many years after. One year, I decided to go all in and run a marathon. I was used to an occasional three mile run when I felt like it, and I just signed up for 26.2 miles! From the moment I put my name on the list, my identity changed. I was no longer a random jogger, I was a marathon runner. Instantly, everything about me was different. I ate differently, slept differently, and thought differently. My priorities were completely rearranged.

I had signed up with a training group, and on the first day of training we met at 7:00 a.m. in the middle of January, which means I also had to learn how to dress differently for running. We were given a five mile and a six mile option for the first run. I immediately decided to go for the five mile, since I hadn't run more than three miles in years and was afraid of finishing way behind everyone else. As I finished my run, I realized that I was the only person who chose the five mile option. There were several people who were slower than me who still chose to go the six miles. I found in that moment that I was still living by my old identity and mindset...when training, never do more than you have to. I realized that I cheated myself out of the full marathon runner experience on that day and vowed to step more fully into my new identity.

As the training continued, I got stronger and faster. I chose to give every workout my best. I also began to discover other aspects of what it means to be a marathon runner. I found that long distance runners are some of the most encouraging people I have ever met. Every person that passed me or that I met as we were doing intervals cheered me on. Every person. Every time. When we were running hills in the dark, you could tell where everyone was by the hoots and cheers you heard as people met each other. I decided I wanted to take on that identity too and delighted in cheering others on. They also were always willing to set aside their own time goals in order to help others who were struggling. I got to add that to the list of things that being a marathon runner meant. I also learned that being a marathon runner meant you weren't deterred by bad weather or getting lost on your run, or struggling with figuring out how to carry your water and nutrition packs for 20 plus miles. When you are a long distance runner, you learn to take all kinds of obstacles in stride (pun intended).

I had signed up with the hopes of being able to say that I ran a marathon, but I came away from the experience with so much more. I discovered a new identity, a new culture, and a new mindset that has stayed with me to this day.

When we put our faith in Christ, most of us did so with the hope of eternal salvation, and certainly that is a wonderful gift, but there is so much more for us! With our salvation comes a completely new identity. We are a new creation! Our old selves no longer exist, but now our lives are intertwined with the life of Christ, and we get to discover who we are now and what that looks and feels like. What an amazing journey of identity Christ has invited us on!

PRAYER

God, I confess that I have trouble seeing myself the way You do. My weaknesses and past experiences can be so tangible, while Your Truth sometimes feels too good to be true. Show me what You see when You look at me. Tell me who I am in You, regardless of my feelings. Thank You for Your unwavering confidence and enthusiasm in who You created me to be. I am ready for my new life adventure with You!

Amen.

REACHING DEEPER

When I began training for a marathon, I had some old mindsets and patterns of behavior that didn't align with my new identity as a marathon runner. It was a beautiful process as I began to discover all of the amazing aspects that go with being a long-distance runner. Tomorrow we will walk through a process of letting go of old identities that no longer belong to us, and grabbing hold of all the amazing aspects of our new identities that come from being a new creation in Christ.

WEEK FIVE

DEEPLY ROOTED IN THE IMAGE OF GOD

WHEN WE DISCOVER OUR UNIQUE AND POWERFUL IDENTITY IN CHRIST

THURSDAY

 ## AN EXERCISE IN GOING DEEPER

Yesterday, we learned that, because of Christ, we are a new creation. We are no longer defined by our past, our weaknesses, or what others say about us. Our true identity comes from God, our Creator, who knew us before we were born.

Today, we are going to go through an exercise of laying down all of the names and identities that have held us back and disqualified us, and we are going to exchange them for our God-given identities.

"You were taught...to put off your old self...to be made new in the attitude of your minds; and to put on the new self, created to be like God in true righteousness and holiness."
(Ephesians 4:22-24)

 # QUESTIONS/ACTIVITIES

1. Think back over your life, and consider all the names, identities, or traits that have been placed on you that you feel are negative or hold you back. Make a list of these names as they come to you. More importantly, write down the things that you think about yourself.

_____

_____

_____

_____

_____

2. Find a quiet place where you can be still *(rapha - let go)* and know *(Yada - touch, hear, experience)* that He is God.

3. Give this list from Question #1 to God. *Rapha* - let it go. These names do not belong to you.

4. Ask God to show you how He sees you. Ask Him to give you His list of who you are. Be aware that what He says about you could very well be in conflict with your experience and the way you think about yourself. (For example, He may say that you are deeply wise, when you have always gotten bad grades in school or felt stupid). Also be aware that if it is negative and makes you feel bad about yourself, it is not from God.

Remember that God sees you fully redeemed through Christ. He is aware of our weaknesses, but He does not define us by them. He calls us by how He sees us and invites us to step into that identity. If what you hear feels too good to be true, in fact so good that you might feel embarrassed or sheepish in writing it down, that is God! He is your biggest fan. He created you, after all, and He knew what He was doing! Write that new list here.

---

5. Return to the list of "Who I am in Christ" in Appendix #Three. Take time to slowly read it out loud. Meditate on the truth of the words as you speak them.

6. Add the things that God showed you in Question #4 to the list in Appendix #Three. Return to this list on a regular basis to read it out loud over yourself, and let God, in His grace and mercy, continue to add to this list of how He thinks about you.

BECOMING DEEPLY ROOTED

"Putting off our old self and putting on our new self" is a process. It takes practice and intentionality. Throughout this week, be attentive to the thoughts and feelings that you have about yourself, especially when you are struggling, when you make mistakes, or when you do something that you've never done before. They may come in thoughts like: *I can't do this, I'm not good enough,* or *I never should have tried this.* They may come in feelings of discouragement, anxiety, or turning down opportunities that you don't feel like you are good enough or capable of doing. Write down those thoughts and experiences, and then bring them before God to get His perspective. God wants to give you new levels of courage, freedom, and confidence by releasing those negative identities you've given yourself. This is the beginning of an amazing new adventure with Him!

PRAYER

Father God, thank You that this is just a small taste of all the things You declare about me. It seems too good to be true, yet You are the TRUTH. Help me understand what these things mean for me and for my life. Show me how to receive these truths into my heart and my mind, so that I may be changed by the power of Your Word and Your Goodness.

Amen.

WEEK FIVE

DEEPLY ROOTED IN THE IMAGE OF GOD

WHEN WE DISCOVER OUR UNIQUE AND POWERFUL IDENTITY IN CHRIST

> *"Life isn't about finding yourself. It's about discovering who God created you to be."*
> *author unknown*

"I will give them a white stone with a new name written on it, known only to the one who receives it."
(Revelation 2:17)

FRIDAY

 A UNIQUE NAME

Did you realize that what makes you different, makes you beautiful to God? Read the verse above from Revelation 2 again. God made you so unique, that He gave you a name no one else has. He created you so special that you can express His heart and reach others in a way that no one else can.

As we learned earlier this week, there are truths about who we are as followers of Christ. They are true to all of us, but there is also an identity given by God only to you. As soon as you put your faith in God, all of those statements we read on Wednesday (as well as countless others) became a part of your new name, but you also received an identity given only to you. There are many biblical examples of God giving new names and new identities to people as He places His call on their lives. Some of these examples include:

Gen. 17:5 Abram to Abraham (meaning Father of Many Nations).

Gen. 32:28. Jacob (meaning Deceiver) to Israel (meaning One Who Wrestles with God).

Jud. 6:12. God calls Gideon "Mighty Warrior."

I Sam. 13:14 God calls David "A man after His own heart."

Matt. 16:16. God changes Simon's name to Peter (meaning Rock).

GIDEON LEARNS HIS NEW NAME

One of my favorite characters in the Bible is Gideon. When we first meet Gideon (in Judges 6:11), he is scared and hiding in a winepress. The Midianites have invaded Israel and are leaving the people poor and hungry, so Gideon is trying to hide his wheat below ground level.

Then an angel of the Lord comes to Gideon and says, "The LORD is with you, *Mighty Warrior.*" This statement completely goes over Gideon's head. God just made a bold statement to Gideon about how He sees him, but it is so far outside the realm of what Gideon thinks about himself, that he completely misses it. He responds, "If you are with us, then why is this happening to us?" So God repeats Himself, "*You* are strong, and I am sending you to free Israel from the Midianites." I can just see His eyes go wide as he spits out some wheat he has been chewing on – half in shock and half in laughter.

This is almost always the response we have when God gives us a new name. Sarah laughed (Genesis 18:12). Moses said, "Who am I?"(Exodus 3:11), and Jeremiah replied "I'm too young!" (Jeremiah 1:6)

Gideon's response was going into a very long list of all that he wasn't, naming every reason he could think of that disqualified him. It's great to see how God completely ignores this list, like He didn't even hear it. God knew Gideon far better than Gideon knew Himself, and He was determined to help him see and believe his true identity.

As the story goes on, we follow Gideon as he takes small steps of faith. One step at a time, he learns to trust that God knew what He was talking about. He learned to trust more and more that

God was truly with him and wasn't going to let him down. He moved from fearfully removing his family's idols in the middle of the night, to taking on the entire army of Midianites with 300 guys, a few jugs of oil, and some horns!

How often do we disqualify ourselves for what God has called us to do? How long are our lists of excuses? How gracious and faithful of a God we have, that He doesn't even listen to all of the negative names we give ourselves, because He knows they are not true! In fact, it is often the areas that we believe are our weakest, that God declares to be our strongest. After all, His power is made most evident in these areas! (2 Cor. 12:9). What could it look like for God to take your greatest weakness and use it to bring Glory to His Name and many people into His Kingdom?

 # BECOMING ROOTED

As we see from Gideon's story, stepping into the unique name that God wants to give us can be a process. It takes time to see ourselves in a new way. It takes being willing to take steps of faith as we learn to believe what God says about us. This is the process of becoming rooted in our unique identity in Christ.

 # PRAYER

Almighty God Who calls the weak and helpless, the broken and disqualified, the unskilled and untrained – You gave me a new name, calling me strong and powerful, whole and effective, bold and fearless. Help me see the unique way You made me.

Help me hear Your voice call me by that name that no one else has. Help me see clearly how You made me and what my purpose is on this earth.

Amen.

 # REACHING DEEPER

Tomorrow, we are going to walk through a process where you begin to explore and discover God's unique name for you. We will learn how to trust that what God says about you is true, as you begin taking steps to intentionally align yourself with what He is showing you.

WEEK FIVE

DEEPLY ROOTED IN THE IMAGE OF GOD

WHEN WE DISCOVER OUR UNIQUE AND POWERFUL IDENTITY IN CHRIST

SATURDAY

 ## AN EXERCISE IN GOING DEEPER

Let's take some time today to consider the unique identity God has given us. This is just the "ice breaker" to a beautiful and life-long conversation with God. Just like our roles in life (child, sibling, parent, grandparent, co-worker, friend, and spouse), this identity will develop and shift throughout our lives. There is no end to the amazing things we can discover with God about who He made us to be and what He is calling us to. This process is driven by the Holy Spirit as He reveals to you all the new and growing aspects of your identity in Him, so let's start with a prayer.

PRAYER

Father God, I confess that I don't always see myself clearly through Your eyes. It is often far easier to listen to the voices around me and my past experiences than it is to listen to – and believe – Your perspective. Open my eyes, my ears, and my heart, Lord, to Your voice, now. Come and show me what You see when You look at me. What was in Your heart that moment You formed me? What weaknesses of mine do You want to declare Your power over? Give me courage to recognize and believe Your voice as You speak to me.

Amen.

QUESTIONS/ACTIVITIES

Some notes to keep in mind while going through this exercise:

- Throughout this exercise, if something comes to your mind that leaves you with any sense of discouragement, hope-lessness or leaves you feeling bad about yourself, THAT IS NOT GOD! That is condemnation. The Holy Spirit has a way of leaving us feeling hopeful and excited about who we are becoming in God, even while convicting us!
- If anything comes to mind that seems too good to be true; that leaves you sheepishly excited and nervous at the same time, or anything that makes you laugh because it seems so ridiculous, THAT IS GOD! We've seen the biblical pattern.

Write those things in **BIG, BOLD LETTERS** and **star them** because that is who God is calling you to be!

- If you don't hear anything right away, that is okay. Thank God that He knows you, and keep on returning to Him to listen throughout the week. The most important part of this entire guide is learning to approach God and just be with Him – no matter the tangible outcome. It is His desire just to spend time with you. The answers will come in His timing and as you learn to develop and nurture this gift of relationship with Him.

1. Take a moment to quiet yourself before the Lord. Ask Him to begin to show you how He sees you. Ask Him to describe you. Write down what you hear.

_____

_____

_____

_____

_____

2. Take a separate sheet of paper to write down any negative thought that comes to mind. Any excuses or thoughts of not being good enough or not having the right gifts should go onto that separate sheet of paper.

3. Think about a time in your life when you felt fulfilled or when you felt like you were right where you were supposed to be in that moment. Write the story here.

_____

_____

_____

_____

_____

4. Think about a time when God blessed somebody else through you. Write that story here.

_____

_____

_____

_____

_____

5. What kind of things are you passionate about? What makes your heart sing? If you can't think of any, that is okay. Ask God to show

you, and then throughout the week, pay attention to the things that grab your heart and attention, and write those things here.

_____

_____

_____

_____

_____

6. Write down a list of names of people who inspire you. They can be biblical, historical, or fictional characters. Some may be people that you know personally. What is it that inspires you about these people? These things point to the type of person God created you to be. We often admire people we wish we were more like. It is God who put that desire in you. He is awakening something in you through other people's stories. What characteristics is He stirring in you through these people?

_____

_____

_____

_____

7. Now for the big, fun question: If you could do anything you wanted in life, knowing that you would always have everything you need to do it and you couldn't fail, what would you do? A lot of times, this aligns with our weaknesses. Areas that we have struggled with are often the exact areas that God wants to use us to bless and help others. Gideon was oppressed by the Midianites and was crying out to God for help, when God showed up and declared that Gideon was going to be the one to defeat this same enemy for the entire nation of Israel. As we consider this question, we find that it points to the passions God has placed in our hearts and what He is calling us to.

\
\
\
\
\

8. Take that separate sheet of paper with your negative thoughts about yourself on it, and rip it up as an offering of faith to God. By that act, you are declaring that you are no longer going to listen to any voice but God's, when it comes to determining who you are.

BECOMING DEEPLY ROOTED

This is a beautiful, life-long process of discovery. This process also requires faith in order for your full identity in Christ to develop and flourish. Faith is necessary in order to believe what God says about us as opposed to the self-defeating thoughts we so often have about ourselves. Continue to keep a list of things that God says about you. If you find that you have difficulty believing these things, then go back to Step #8. As you continue this practice of agreeing with what God says and intentionally letting go of the negative things you believe about yourself, you will become deeply rooted in your true identity in Christ.

PRAYER

God, I again give You all of this process and ask that You continue to draw me close and show me who You made me to be. Thank You that You delight in me and that You call me Your own. Thank You for Your power that overrides all of my weaknesses, that I may show others what an amazing, loving, and powerful God You are.

Amen.

WEEK SIX

DEEPLY ROOTED AS THE PEOPLE OF GOD

WHEN WE BECOME GOOD NEWS TO THE WORLD AROUND US

WEEK SIX

DEEPLY ROOTED AS THE PEOPLE OF GOD

WHEN WE BECOME GOOD NEWS TO THE WORLD AROUND US

> *"Being filled with the Spirit is simply this - having my whole nature yielded to His power. When the whole soul is yielded to the Holy Spirit, God Himself will fill it."*
> *Andrew Murray*

MONDAY

 EMPOWERED BY THE
HOLY SPIRIT

*"I am going to send you what my Father has promised; but
stay in the city until you have been clothed with power
from on high." When he had led them out to the vicinity
of Bethany, he lifted up his hands and blessed them. While
he was blessing them, he left them and was taken up into
heaven. Then they worshiped him and returned to Jerusalem
with great joy." (Luke 24:49-52)*

This is how Jesus left His disciples. They had been living life
together for a few years now. They had literally walked with God,
in the form of Jesus, learning from Him while they followed Him.
They were obedient to His command to go to Jerusalem and wait,
but they were still a little lost and confused. They had been waiting in a room together, worshiping and praying in unity, but they
were not yet fully the Church.

We are often in this place. We know what it is we are *supposed* to be doing, but it seems at times lifeless and meaning-
less. We don't know what God is up to. We don't understand
the seasons of waiting. And sometimes we give up the waiting
and turn to our own devices. We try to move on with life the
best we can. But for those who continue through those waiting
seasons, the best is yet to come! It is the gift of the Holy Spirit!
It is in those moments in God's presence that we are radically
changed forever. It is in this moment that these twelve lost and

confused guys became "those that have turned the world up-side down!" (Acts 17:6)

> "When the day of Pentecost came, they were all together in one place. Suddenly a sound like the blowing of a violent wind came from heaven and filled the whole house where they were sitting. They saw what seemed to be tongues of fire that separated and came to rest on each of them. All of them were filled with the Holy Spirit and began to speak in other tongues as the Spirit enabled them."
> (Acts 2:1-4)

It's worth the waiting! Much like the disciples' experience at Pentecost, we can be blessed with the power and presence of God when we wait on Him expectantly, as they did.

 WHEN THE HOLY SPIRIT CAME TO SCHOOL

I experienced something like this at my first true community revival while I was a college student at Hope College in Michigan. The college held an elective chapel three days a week, but to be honest, I didn't even know it existed until my Junior year when I met a couple of the twenty or so students that attended chapel services. Although it was founded as a Christian college, actual Jesus-loving students were kind of hard to find. In my senior year, the college hired a new team to lead the chapel. This included a chaplain who was in tune with the Holy Spirit and passionate about sharing God's heart, as well as a worship leader who understood the difference between singing songs and true praise and worship. It didn't take long before the average crowd of twenty turned into an average crowd of 400. People are attracted to passionate people. For many churches, this would be their dream – find some charismatic leaders, update the music, and draw a huge crowd in. But the Holy Spirit had so much more for that small college, and He has so much more for us as His Bride than what we can do with our own talents and charisma!

During Spring Break, I went on a mission trip with some fellow students who all attended the same Spirit sensitive church. We had a wonderful time of serving and growing, but during that time, the Holy Spirit kept calling us to pray. In fact, on our fifteen-hour drive back home, we all prayed in unity the entire time for our school – something that only the Holy Spirit could do! When we returned to school, we could tell that God was up to something big, but we had no idea what. We could feel the air filled with electricity.

We kept gathering together and praying. Two weeks later, during a Sunday evening service at the chapel, the chaplain stood up and said that he felt God wanted to do something, and he didn't want to get in the way. He then encouraged us to wait on God together, and he went to sit down in a pew (after looking at our group and mouthing, *PRAY!*) He knew he was taking a huge spiritual and career risk by making this move, but he had chosen to place his trust totally in God! We prayed and looked around and waited together for about ten minutes, not knowing what was going to happen or what to do. Nobody moved.

Then one person bolted out of his seat and to the front, like he was being catapulted there – and confessed a pretty serious sin. For a moment, we were all a little stunned. Then teams ran up to pray for him. One minute later, another person came up to confess, then another, then another, then there was a line out the door! Until 2:00 a.m., people were confessing, repenting, and being prayed for, and there was still a line out the door! The chaplain decided to close in prayer and call a meeting again for the next night, and the same thing happened! For four nights in a row, there was non-stop repentance, confession, and prayer. By the fifth night, the chaplain had called for a night of praise and thanksgiving for all God had done! In that week, the chapel attendance grew from 400 to thousands! It was standing room only! People were crowding in the aisles and out the doors!

The worship and praise filled the city, and many local congregations were affected! The following year, the number of Bible studies and small groups that took place in the dorms was in the hundreds! (There had not been a single group prior to this time!) In fact, decades later, that college is a completely different place. Both the chaplain and worship leader are long gone, but the chapel and Sunday service are still standing room only. People still come from all over the region to be a part of this move of God, and more importantly, imagine all the students who have met God there in a powerful way and have gone on to share Him with others all over the world!

BECOMING ROOTED

Growing up in the Midwest, I have come to love the month of March. After a long, harsh winter, I knew that when March arrived, Spring was close. There were usually very few signs of Spring on the first of the month, yet hope and eager expectation would begin to grow in my heart. Spring was going to come. There was no doubt about it, no matter how long the winter may linger.

We also go through different seasons in our spiritual lives. There are seasons of difficulties and times when it seems like nothing is happening. These are our seasons of waiting. But there is something we can be sure of. God has more in store for us than we can possibly imagine! In these seasons, we can set our eyes on Him and wait with eager anticipation for all of His promises to come to fulfillment. There is no doubt about it. When we wait expectantly on God, we will be blessed by the power and the presence of the Holy Spirit, and we will be transformed into people who turn the world upside down for the sake of Christ.

 **PRAYER**

Holy Spirit, I am so grateful for Your presence in my life! I lay down my own plans, agendas, and strength so that You can move freely in my life. Open my eyes and ears to be more sensitive to Your leading, and give me the courage to trust You completely!

Amen.

 **REACHING DEEPER**

Tomorrow we will take a closer look at three keys to positioning ourselves for a transformational encounter with the Holy Spirit.

WEEK SIX

DEEPLY ROOTED AS THE PEOPLE OF GOD

WHEN WE BECOME GOOD NEWS TO THE WORLD AROUND US

TUESDAY

 ## AN EXERCISE IN GOING DEEPER

There are three keys in both of these stories that will position us for a Pentecostal type move of God in our lives and in our church communities:

- Waiting on God
- Prayer
- Being together in Unity

Before I go on to these three keys, I want to be clear about one thing: If you have received Christ as your Savior, the Holy Spirit is already living inside you. You don't have to beg, or say the right things, or hope it's true. It is a gift you have been given. What has happened, though, is that many of us who grew up in church never really heard much about the Holy Spirit or what living a life empowered by the Holy Spirit looks like. Many of us read the stories about Pentecost and all the miracles that happened in the book of Acts, and we thought that was just a special time or just for special people, when in fact, Christ said that we would do even greater things than He did because of this precious gift of the Holy Spirit. In many churches, the Holy Spirit is thought of as some kind of weird uncle you don't talk about and that you tuck in the back room during parties. The truth is that the Holy Spirit is living in us, and we get to choose on a daily basis whether or not to actively and intentionally engage Him. The Holy Spirit is the most helpful, encouraging, empowering, and wise person I know, and we get to continue to learn to listen and be attentive to all that He wants to show us, teach us, and do through us.

Imagine the impact that just a handful of people made on the world when they were filled with the Holy Spirit. What kind of impact could you have on the world with that same Spirit living inside you? You can't dream big enough! (Eph. 3:20). We just have to be willing, like the disciples, to wait and pray together, and we will be the ones impacting the world by the power of the Holy Spirit.

 **QUESTIONS/ACTIVITIES**

KEY #1: Waiting on God

"But wait in Jerusalem until you have been clothed with power from on high." (Luke 24:49)

Waiting for the Lord is a common theme throughout scripture, but what does it mean to wait? What does waiting on God look like?

Waiting on God is not passive. It does not mean that we binge on Netflix until God does something. Waiting on God requires stillness, patience, and listening for His still, small voice. Worship can be very helpful in the waiting. It places our eyes on God instead of our problem. It can be very tempting in the face of a problem to try to solve it in our own strength. It can feel like a waste of time to sit quietly and listen while there are fires to put out. This takes practice. This takes trust, but would you rather influence 400 people you got in your own strength or the decades of standing room only that the Holy Spirit can bring in His power?

1. Find a quiet place where you can be still.

2. Think about the things that you most long for and write them here.

_____

_____

_____

_____

_____

3. Offer these things to Jesus. He knows you and cares about you more than you could ever imagine. Trust Him with the things on your heart.

4. Take 5 minutes to sit quietly and wait for Him.

5. Ask Him to show you what is on His heart for this situation, and then be still and listen. If you are not hearing anything, then just be with Him. Sit quietly with Him and wait for His timing.

   (Just a little heads up; He sometimes LOVES to wait until what seems to us as the last minute. It grows our trust in Him and lengthens His time with us, which He relishes. Don't be discouraged if it takes some time. He is changing you in the waiting, and He will never let you down!)

6. Write down the things God shows you or what your time of waiting with Him was like.

_____

_____

_____

_____

_____

_____

_____

KEY #2: Prayer

"They all joined together constantly in prayer."
(Acts 1:14)

After Jesus told the disciples to wait in Jerusalem, they gathered together and prayed constantly. This was not just a *God-bless-me-as-I-go-about-my-day-today* kind of prayer. This was a prayer in the waiting. Moses prayed this kind of prayer in Exodus 33:15-16 when He said to God that He would not leave that spot unless God's presence would go with them. In fact, He continued on by saying that if they (the Israelites) left there without God's presence, then nothing would distinguish them from the rest of the world.

This is a Pentecostal prayer. I wonder how different I am from the rest of the world. I wonder if those who meet me immediately think, *She has been with Jesus*, like the world recognized the disciples after that day. (Acts 4:13) The world can see the difference between a religious person living by all the proper Christian rules, and someone who spends their time with the person of Jesus. They can see the difference between a good Sunday service and something that is real and powerful and life changing. Only the power of the Holy Spirit can transform us from disciples into world changers. Only He can cause the light of Christ to shine so brightly within us that something truly different is seen in us. We cannot make that happen in our own strength. It is the presence of God in us. Are you willing to cry out to God for more of Him and less of you in your life? If so, set aside some time today to pray.

1. Ask the Holy Spirit to fill you daily, and ask God to make you increasingly sensitive to the voice and leading of the Holy Spirit.

2. Continue to practice listening. Take note of scriptures, words, and people that come to mind here.

_____

_____

_____

_____

_____

3. The most beautiful truth I have learned about prayer is that we get to pray *with* God instead of *toward* God. Jesus and the Holy Spirit are constantly praying for us. We get to listen in on their prayers and join them, knowing that all of our prayers will be answered because it is what God is praying! Take time to ask God what He is praying for in your life and the lives of those around you. What is on His heart? Write down here the things that He shows you.

_____

_____

_____

_____

_____

*"For everyone who asks receives; the one who seeks finds; and
to the one who knocks, the door will be opened."*
(Matt. 7:8)

KEY #3: Unity

"They were all together in one place."
(Acts 2:1)

I had the amazing blessing of joining *Youth With A Mission*
(YWAM) on a summer mission at the '96 Summer Olympics in
Atlanta, Georgia. I cannot adequately describe the glimpse of
Heaven that I had at the beginning of each day as 5,000 kids and
young adults from over 200 different countries joined together to
worship. We were led in worship in a multitude of cultures and
languages. We worshiped to songs we all knew, each in our own
language, yet all one in the Spirit. Some of you might remember
that a bomb was set off during this time with two deaths and well
over one hundred casualties. Imagine a crowd of 5,000 people
from around the world joining together in prayer at the bomb site,
praying in Korean, English, Spanish, German, French, and countless other different languages, dialects and prayer styles – all as
one, lifting our voices in prayer!

How beautiful it is to God to see His children from all different cultures and viewpoints lay aside their differences in order to
seek His face! How powerful! What a testimony it is to the rest of
the world when we demonstrate true love for one another! After
all, Christ said that the world will know that we are His followers
by the way we love each other.

This kind of love is not easy. It can require an incredible
amount of humility and self-sacrifice. Jesus describes this kind of

radical love in Matthew 5:43 when He commands us to love our enemies and pray for those who persecute us. This is not a human kind of love. This is the kind of love that compelled Jesus to suffer and die for those who were against Him. This is the kind of love that only God can give.

1. Take a moment to think about a person or a group of people that is the hardest for you to love. Write down that person or group here.

_____

_____

_____

2. Ask God to show you how He sees that person or group. Write down what He shows you.

_____

_____

_____

_____

_____

_____

3. Ask God to show you what He loves about them. Write that down here.

_____

_____

_____

_____

_____

4. Begin to ask God to fill you with His love and compassion for them. What does His love for them feel like?

_____

_____

_____

_____

_____

5. Write down your experiences with God's heart for that person or group.

_____

_____

_____

_____

_____

6. Once you start to experience God's heart for that person or group, continue to pray this way, and ask God to show you how you can share His love with them, and then do that. Write down what He shows you here as well as what occurs with them and within you during any interactions you might have.

_____

_____

_____

_____

_____

BECOMING DEEPLY ROOTED

It is no surprise that the world is being increasingly ripped apart by divisions. It is not in our nature to love our enemies. It is in our nature to protect ourselves and to strengthen that sense of protection by aligning with those who agree with us. It is human nature. But it is NOT in God's nature.

"You see, at just the right time, when we were still powerless, Christ died for the ungodly. Very rarely will anyone die for a righteous person, though for a good person someone might possibly dare to die. But God demonstrates His own love for us in this: While we were still sinners, Christ died for us."
(Romans 5:6-8)

I believe that nothing transforms us into the image of Christ faster than learning how to truly love our enemies. It is the kind of love that sets itself apart from the rest of the world. It is the kind of love that shines in the darkness like a city on a hill. It is the kind of love that can only come from God. And it is the kind of love that we have freely received so that we can freely give it away.

 **PRAYER**

Jesus, there is no greater miracle than the overwhelming love You have lavished on me. Open my heart to fully receive the height, the width, and the depths of Your love for me. Fill me to overflowing with this love and cause it to pour out of me onto everyone around me. Open my eyes to see those around me the way you see them, and open my heart to love even the most difficult people in my life with Your love. Make me more like you.

Amen.

WEEK SIX

DEEPLY ROOTED AS THE PEOPLE OF GOD

WHEN WE BECOME GOOD NEWS TO THE WORLD AROUND US

> *"If the Kingdom of God is in you,*
> *you should leave a little bit*
> *of heaven wherever you go."*
> Cornel West

"As you go, proclaim this message:
'The Kingdom of heaven has come near.'"
(Matthew 10:7)

WEDNESDAY

PROCLAIMERS OF THE KINGDOM

The words we speak carry weight and power. We proclaim something every time we open our mouths. We impart something. We affect the atmosphere around us. Have you ever been going about your day when someone passes you on the road, shouting at you and giving you the finger? Suddenly your mood changes, and you begin to feel a little agitated or grumpy – or even hurt. Consider the last time someone gave you a compliment that completely changed how you felt about yourself in that moment? Suddenly, you walked a little taller and smiled a little brighter.

Throughout the Gospels, Jesus frequently talks about "Proclaiming the Kingdom." But what does that mean? What does that look like and sound like?

We have a beautiful explanation of what it looks like to proclaim the Kingdom in Luke 4:18-19. Jesus becomes our perfect example once again as He stands up and declares:

*"The Spirit of the Lord is on me, because he has anointed me to **proclaim** good news to the poor. He has sent me to **proclaim** freedom for the prisoners and recovery of sight for the blind, to set the oppressed free, to **proclaim** the year of the Lord's favor."*

THE KINGDOM WAS PROCLAIMED TO ME

I endured a lot of trauma and abuse growing up. As a result, I quickly became very quiet and shut off. I barely spoke. In fact, for a couple of years I decided not to speak at all, because I thought if people forgot I was there, they would not hurt me anymore. On top of this, my anxiety about facing daily life was so intense, that I would throw up every morning at some point before going to school – or on the bus – or in the halls at school. *Every Day. For 8 years.* Some teachers eventually persuaded my parents to put me on a mild tranquilizer to help this, but I was already broken. For me, getting actual help was out of my reach, and I was invisible to the world. These things do not help one's social life. As the years went on, the friends I did have began to ditch me, because I was too quiet or had a sick smell to me. One by one, they disappeared. Today they call this *ghosting*, which is an appropriate term, because that is what I felt like – a ghost. No one could see me. No one could hear me. I walked the halls of school alone, hid in the bathroom during breaks, and sat alone on the floor by my locker to eat my lunch – a ghost.

I am beyond grateful for the grace of Jesus on me during this time. As a small child, Jesus was my only playmate. As I grew up, He was often the only Person I spoke to, and the only One Who actually spoke to me. Jesus was truly my best, and only, friend and I learned a lot about His heart, His kindness, His voice, and His love for me during these years of deep suffering.

My Senior year in High School, I took a Pre-calculous class with a teacher named Mr. VanDyke. Mr. VanDyke was a nice and well-liked teacher, like many I have had through the years. At first, I did well in his class, but then we had a student teacher take over that I couldn't understand at all. I started getting D's on all the tests, and I really struggled. Through this time, Mr. VanDyke started smiling at me when I passed him in the hall. He would smile and say, "Hi, Stacey!" (Like he was actually happy to see me, when no one else saw me at all.)

On a particularly rough day, a few moments after I had just found out my grandpa had passed away, I was trying to gather my books from my locker without completely falling apart. He came out of his room and knelt right beside me. He asked me how my day was going and if I was okay. I mumbled something about having a rough day and walked off, but it was the first time anyone had ever asked me if I was okay, and it started to shift something in me.

His kindness gave me strength in that difficult moment. Towards the end of the semester, our student teacher left our class, and Mr. VanDyke was back to teaching. Our class was filled with students I liked and respected, although, of course, I never really spoke to them. One day, Mr. VanDyke was handing back our first graded tests since he returned to teaching the class. As he moved towards the center of the room, he said "I have an announcement!" (He'd never done anything like this before.) "We have a Pre-calculous wiz in our class! The highest grade belongs to – Stacey!" He started smiling and clapping, and the whole room erupted in cheers! I am sure my face turned red at all the attention, as students genuinely cheered me on, saying things like, "Way to go, Smarty!" and "You need to teach me your skills!" with some even patting me on the back. I am sure that neither Mr. VanDyke nor anyone else in that class remembers this moment, but for me, this was one of the highlights of my young life, and it had nothing to do with the grade.

For the first time in my life, I was lifted up instead of pushed down. I was seen and not assaulted. I was encouraged and not used. I don't know where Mr. VanDyke is now. He never knew how huge an impact his kindness and his words had on me. Yet this is sometimes what it is like when you are a proclaimer of the Kingdom. You may never know the power that a kind word has on someone's life, but I promise you that it does.

> *"The Spirit of the Lord is on me, because he has anointed me to **proclaim** good news to the poor. He has sent me to **proclaim** freedom for the prisoners and recovery of sight for the blind, to set the oppressed free, to **proclaim** the year of the Lord's favor."*

Mr. VanDyke was Good News to me. His kindness and his words brought release to this broken and lonely girl. He stood up and proclaimed to a class full of people that I was valuable, appreciated, seen, and enjoyed, and in so doing, proclaimed life and freedom over me. I felt like I was no longer a ghost after that day. I started to become a person. Some of the old friends that had long since "disappeared" on me were in that classroom, and those friendships were restored. I grew in inner strength and self-confidence. I began to break free from my prison of isolation.

How amazing and humbling a gift to be able to affect someone's life so powerfully with just a few simple words!

How do we learn to do this in our own lives? First, we need to go back to the Holy Spirit. Jesus was able to perfectly proclaim the Kingdom because of His oneness and perfect relationship with the Holy Spirit. He was anointed by the Father, through the Holy Spirit, to proclaim Good News – and to *be* Good News.

The second key is found in John 12:49-50.

> *"I do not speak on my own, but the Father who sent me commanded me to say all that I have spoken. I know that his command leads to eternal life. So whatever I say is just what the Father has told me to say."*

What a beautiful moment it is when God whispers in your ear to tell someone He loves them, to give them a word of encouragement, to proclaim to them how God sees them, and to be Good News from God to someone who is in need of Good News.

 # BECOMING ROOTED

If you were to walk through an orchard in the summer or early fall, you would be able to tell what kind of tree you were looking at by the fruit on the tree. It is the same thing with our words. Luke 6:45 states *"...for the mouth speaks what the heart is full of."* What is it that you talk about most often? What takes up your thoughts? What do you share or post about on social media? These are the things that we proclaim. We become proclaimers of the Kingdom when we let our thoughts and hearts be consumed with Jesus and the Kingdom of heaven that He came to release among us. And what an overwhelming love and astounding Kingdom it is!

PRAYER

Jesus, thank You for being Good News in my life. Thank You for the freeing power of Your Word and Your heart spoken over me. Help me to be Good News to someone today. Tell me, by Your Spirit, what I should say and how to say it. Make me bold in proclaiming Good News to those around me, so that those imprisoned by the words and actions of others can be free – and so those weighed down under darkness and hopelessness can find light and joy in You. Cause those who have been cast aside and deemed unworthy in the eyes of the world to be raised up by Your overflowing favor.

Amen.

REACHING DEEPER

Tomorrow we will go through an exercise where we will learn how to proclaim the Kingdom over the life of someone God has trusted you with for just this purpose.

WEEK SIX

DEEPLY ROOTED AS THE PEOPLE OF GOD

WHEN WE BECOME GOOD NEWS TO THE WORLD AROUND US

THURSDAY

 **AN EXERCISE IN GOING DEEPER**

"God does not ask us to call people out on their sin. He asks us to speak to the person God created them to be and call them up into that fullness of life." (Well-known author, speaker, friend of God, and spiritual mentor, Graham Cooke).

It can be easy to look at someone and judge them by the way they look, dress, act, and speak. It takes the Holy Spirit in us to see a person the way God sees them.

"For God does not look at the things people look at. People look at the outward appearance, but God looks at the heart."
(I Sam. 16:7)

We cannot truly see another person's heart without looking through God's eyes. We cannot know what someone else is experiencing or, more importantly, what God sees when He looks at that person through the redeeming work of Christ. When God created each one of us, He saw our uniqueness, our gifts, and the ways we were created to display His heart and His image. Sometimes that person that God sees can get buried underneath the pain, hurt, and brokenness of this world. It is our immense blessing to call that person forth in others, to lift them up into freedom and healing, to say to someone, "This is you. This is the beautiful gift that you are." God delights in His creation and calls it good. We can proclaim that goodness into the lives of those around us.

 # QUESTIONS/ACTIVITIES

1. Ask God to show you someone in your life that needs to hear Good News. Write that person's name here.

_____

_____

_____

_____

2. Now, ask Him to show you how He sees that person. Write what He shows you here.

_____

_____

_____

_____

_____

3. Ask God what He loves about that person. Write down what He shows you.

_____

_____

_____

_____

_____

4. Ask God to show you who He created them to be. What was on God's heart when He formed that person? Write those things down.

_____

_____

_____

_____

_____

5. Pray for that person, and reach out to them. Send a note to let them know you are thinking about them. Share with them the things God shared with you about them. Give them a word of encouragement. I truly believe that the gift of encouragement is one of the most powerful gifts in Christianity, and it is a gift we all have the ability to give.

6. Write down what you did and how it went. Remember, you may not know how impactful your words were, but if they came from the loving heart of God, I promise you they changed that person's day, if not their life.

_____

_____

_____

_____

_____

7. Maybe you are feeling like that lost, broken, or worthless person, yourself. Listen to God's heart for you. Hear His joy over who He created you to be. Let Him tell you all the things that He loves about you. Feel His unquenchable delight over you. Open yourself up to His love, and be lifted up into His arms. Write down here the things that God loves about you and what He shares with you.

_____

_____

_____

_____

_____

BECOMING DEEPLY ROOTED

As we practice seeing others through God's eyes instead of the world's, the more we will become like Christ. God's heart is full of love, joy, hope and patience when He looks at us. How wonderful that we have been given the opportunity to share in His heart! Think about how powerfully we can touch the lives around us as we learn to proclaim His heart and His Kingdom to them!

 **PRAYER**

God, thank You so much for seeing me differently than the world sees me. Thank You that You delight over me and You adore who You made me to be. Help me to only hear Your voice over me, and help me to only hear Your voice over those around me. Cause me to become a person who proclaims Your heart and Your Kingdom everywhere I go and over everyone I meet. Overwhelm me with Your love.

Amen.

WEEK SIX

DEEPLY ROOTED AS THE PEOPLE OF GOD

WHEN WE BECOME GOOD NEWS TO THE WORLD AROUND US

"The Spirit-filled life is not a special, deluxe edition of Christianity. It is part and parcel of the total plan of God for His people"
A.W. Tozer

"For I did not come to you with wise and persuasive words, but with a demonstration of the Spirit's power, so that your faith might not rest on human wisdom, but on God's power."
(I Cor. 2:4-5)

FRIDAY

DEMONSTRATORS OF THE KINGDOM

Let's take another look at what the Kingdom looks like. In Matthew 11, John the Baptizer was in prison and awaiting execution on account of Christ. In his moment of fear and doubt, he sent some of Jesus' disciples to ask Jesus if He really was the Messiah. This is Christ's reply, "Go back and report what you hear and see: The blind receive sight, the lame walk, those who have leprosy are cleansed, the deaf hear, the dead are raised, and the good news is proclaimed to the poor." (Matt. 11:4-5)

This is what the Kingdom looks like! This is the life Christ demonstrated to us, and this is our calling! How much better a call this is than to just make it through a Sunday morning service once a week and to try to crack our Bibles open once in a while! What if, wherever we go, people are healed, the blind receive their sight, the lame walk, and the dead are raised! This calling does not depend on our ability to convince other people why we believe what we do. It is a testimony that overcomes (Rev. 12:11) and breaks through defenses. I was lonely, and God was my friend. I was wounded, and God healed my heart. I was in a lot of physical pain and unable to walk, and God healed me. Now, by His Spirit, God wants to use me to demonstrate His Kingdom to those around me! What an unbelievable, amazing life we get to have!

WHEN A DEMONSTRATION OF THE KINGDOM TURNED A COUNTRY UPSIDE-DOWN

I had the blessing of going to India to put on an outdoor meeting to share the Gospel there. There were a couple dozen of us West Michiganders, none of us special or particularly gifted in any way, but God had an amazing plan. The Holy Spirit had given us new names and was working through us. Through that week, almost 100,000 people gave their lives to Christ. Starting at about the second night, **every** person who was prayed for was healed. We saw the lame walk and the deaf hear. Many people were delivered. Children were loved on. It was so powerful, that we read in the paper on the flight home that a radical Hindu sect (who also had put up our pictures during the week we were there with a call for assassination, and who had also fire bombed our tents during the night while we were at our hotel) had declared it illegal to receive prayer for healing from a Christian! That is the power of the Holy Spirit at work in a handful of untrained, un-gifted Midwesterners! The world was turned upside down! That same life is available to all of us, for we all have the same Spirit at work in us!

In fact, Jesus said, "On this rock, (giving Peter his new name) I will build my church and the gates of hell will not prevail against it."

Sometimes we read this and think it means that the enemy cannot beat us, but let's read that verse again. "The **gates** of hell will not prevail **against** it." This does not just mean that we are protected against the attacks of the enemy. It means that the enemy **is not safe against us**! The image here is of a

204

church crashing down the gates of hell and running in to save those that have been held prisoner there! We are meant to run into the hellish places of the world with the Gospel and turn everything around! What amazing grace and power is that? What unfathomable calling! ALL OF US! Not just pastors and missionaries. Not just those that have gone to Bible College. Not just those who have been Christians for a long time. If you have put your faith in Christ, this is what your life is meant to look like! It is time we relinquish our small dreams of an uneventful day and a balanced budget – and run full on into the radical life we were called to live – healing the sick, delivering the possessed, saving the lost and bringing wholeness to the broken. We were created to carry that life-giving message of the Gospel of Jesus!

 # BECOMING ROOTED

"Then the angel showed me the river of the water of life, as clear as crystal, flowing from the throne of God and of the Lamb down the middle of the great street of the city. On each side of the river stood the tree of life, bearing twelve crops of fruit, yielding its fruit every month. And the leaves of the tree are for the healing of the nations." (Revelation 22:1-2)

The Kingdom in its fullness is a Kingdom of healing, of wholeness, of abundance, of fruit, and of seeing and loving our Lord face to face. That Kingdom is near. That Kingdom has come to us with the grace of Jesus. That Kingdom is here. It lives in every person that has given their life to Christ. It lives in you.

 # PRAYER

Holy Spirit, I am so grateful that You have come to make my life ASTOUNDING. It is Your desire to connect me more deeply with Jesus and to make me more like Him, and it is my greatest desire as well. Open my eyes to what life in Your Kingdom looks like, and empower me in the ways that the Father created me to be, with a unique and powerful calling that sees Your Kingdom come on earth as it is in Heaven. Make me more sensitive to your voice and your direction in my life, and make me more like Jesus.

Amen.

 # REACHING DEEPER

Tomorrow, we will be taking a look back over these last six weeks in order to get a greater understanding of who God has called you to be and how He is calling you to be a demonstrator of His Kingdom, right where He has placed you.

WEEK SIX

DEEPLY ROOTED AS THE PEOPLE OF GOD

WHEN WE BECOME GOOD NEWS TO THE WORLD AROUND US

SATURDAY

 ## AN EXERCISE IN GOING DEEPER

The picture of the early church in the book of Acts, traveling around the known world, proclaiming and demonstrating the Kingdom with healings, signs, and miracles, can feel so far away from our normal everyday life, that it may seem like a fantasy. I have experienced the power of demonstrating the Kingdom personally, and it still seems dramatically far away from my everyday life of bills and chores. The fact is that we can't heal anyone on our own. We can't make miracles happen. We can't heal a broken heart. Only God can do these things, but God WANTS to do these things through us. He loves to let us join Him in His mission to reach others with His love. There are some things that we can do to learn how to partner with Him in the demonstration of the Kingdom, and together, we have already begun this journey!

 # QUESTIONS/ACTIVITIES

1. Week One, we looked at what God is like. Who has He been for you? This is where we begin. What is your story? Where did God bring healing, provision, and compassion into your life? The Bible is filled with stories of people's encounters with God. No two people and no two encounters are the same. Those stories do not end at the end of the Bible. We each have our own story to tell, and it is important. Your story displays the image and the heart of God in a way that no one else's story can. Your story is there to touch someone in a way that no one else can. Someone needs your God story! Take some time to think about and write down your own story of God in your life. Write down what God has done for you personally. How has knowing Him changed your life? Often the thing that God has healed you from or freed you from is the very thing He has empowered you to heal or free someone else from by His Spirit.

_____

_____

_____

---

2. Week Two, we began to learn how to hear God's voice. Jesus only said what He heard the Father saying and only did what He saw the Father doing – no more, and no less. We don't have to run ourselves ragged trying to do everything and save everyone. We also don't have to keep our heads down and hope someone will somehow see God in us. God has a perfect plan and perfect timing. We have the amazing opportunity to learn how to hear His voice and follow His leading.

Sometimes that means pulling away to rest and spend time in prayer. Sometimes that means sitting quietly next to someone who is hurting. Sometimes it means giving a friendly smile to the cashier at the grocery store. Sometimes it means praying for healing for someone. Sometimes it means doing something bold and crazy like speaking to the waves to be still.

Practice listening. What does God want to talk to you about? Is there someone He wants you to pray for or send a note to? We get to learn to listen and to obey, one small step at a time. God promises that if we are faithful with the small things, our faith, and the way we demonstrate the Kingdom, will grow! Write down the people that come to mind and how God is asking you to join Him in reaching them and loving on them. Write down what you hear and how it went.

_____

_____

_____

_____

_____

3. Week Three, we learned about how to lean on the promises of
    God. This is not only essential for when we are going through
    difficulties, but it is also what we learn to stand on when we are
    learning how to step outside our comfort zones and do some-
    thing we have never done before. It is quite probable if, for
    example, God has given you a specific word of encouragement
    for someone you don't personally know very well, you are going
    to find yourself feeling nervous, unsure, and second guessing
    whether or not you should share it. I have often found myself
    in this place, and still do. I often think, _Why don't I just pray_
    for them? Maybe I can pray that God tells them Himself. Wouldn't
    that be better, anyway? One of the easiest traps we fall into is
    when we take what we hear and water it down into something
    that seems manageable for us. Unfortunately, when we do
    this, we rationalize God out of the situation. We risk less, and
    so we don't end up seeing the full majesty and miracles of His
    Kingdom. It is in this moment of fear between hearing and
    obeying that we need to cling to God's promises the most. It is
    in this moment that we need to remind ourselves how amaz-
    ing our God really is, and stand firmly on His Word and His
    heart. What promises do you need to remember? Feel free to

go back to the list in Appendix #two and find some new promises to stand on as you seek to become a demonstrator of the Kingdom. Perhaps there is a story in the Bible that helps you trust God to be there for you as you step out in faith. Maybe there are other promises that are not listed in this chapter that speak to you. Write them here.

_____

_____

_____

_____

_____

4. Week Four, we learned how to abide in the presence of God. We learned how to stay connected to His presence and listen for His voice throughout the day and not just for a couple of minutes when we get up or before we go to bed. It is as we move through our day that we come in contact with others who need to know God's heart for them. It is in coming up against the obstacles in our day that the opportunity arises to look for how God wants to show up.

I can't tell you the number of times in my day-to-day life I have prayed over broken down cars, computers on the fritz, or people with headaches, sore backs, and other ailments. Sometimes it takes a mechanic, tech person, or aspirin to alleviate the situation, but many times, the car has started up with a prayer, the computer started working again, or the person started to feel better. These situations demonstrated the Gospel to those around me. After a while, you might find that people you live life with, even non-Christians, start to come to you for prayer when they aren't feeling great or things aren't going well in their lives. At this point, your way of life becomes a powerful testimony of God's heart and His power to those around you!

A friend of mine once told me a story about someone she had taken a class with on how to hear God's voice. After the class, this woman was driving home, praying, and thinking about all she had learned. As she was driving, she passed a 7-11 Store and felt an overwhelming sense that she was supposed to go into the store and do a handstand by the Slushy machine. She laughed it off as a silly thought and kept driving, but she couldn't shake the feeling. Eventually, she decided to turn around and do it. What could it hurt? She would just look ridiculous, and she didn't know anyone in that town anyway. She decided that learning to hear God's voice was worth looking stupid, so she went into the store, looked around, was glad to see that no one was in there except for the cashier, did a quick handstand by the Slushy machine, and started to quickly sneak back out the door.

"WHAT DID YOU JUST DO?" yelled the cashier. She shrugged and mumbled, "Ahh, just a handstand." "WHY DID YOU DO THAT?" he demanded. "Um, well, it's silly. I, uh, was just taking a class on hearing God's voice and just thought maybe God was telling me to do a handstand by the Slushy machine. I know it's crazy," as she continued to try to slink out the door. By this time, the cashier was visibly shaken. He took a gun out from behind his register and placed it on the counter. She froze. He went on to tell this woman that he had fully planned to go to work, finish his shift, drive to a nearby field, and kill himself, that day. In a last-ditch grasp for hope, he had told God that if God really existed, He would be able to make someone come in and do a handstand by the Slushy machine! She then was able to share God's heart with this man and lead him to Christ! A silly risk she was willing to take in learning to hear God's voice saved a man's life and soul!

Keep practicing His presence like this woman did. Keep turning your ear and your attention to Him throughout your day. When someone is sharing something with you, practice listening to them and the Holy Spirit, at the same time. There is a reason I keep using the word practice. It takes intentionality to learn how to stay in God's presence – to learn how to keep hold of His hand and let Him lead you throughout the hustle and bustle of your day. Believe me – it is so incredibly worth it! I suggest you start a journal of the little thoughts and nudges you receive from God throughout the day, as well as your response to them. It can be written or recorded or in whatever form works best for you, but as you start to see how He is with you and how He speaks to you, I guarantee you will grow in Him in ways you never imagined!

5. Week Five, we learned about how to see ourselves the way God sees us and how to see others the way God sees them. God has given each of us gifts and callings to help us share His image with those around us. Go back to Week Five, especially the Saturday worksheet, and write down the things God shared with you about how He sees you and who He made you to be.

_____

_____

_____

_____

_____

6. Week Six, we learned how to partner with the Holy Spirit in order to bring the Kingdom of Heaven to those around us. Take some time to ask Him to show you more about who He created you to be in light of being a proclaimer and demonstrator of the Kingdom. What are the spiritual passions that He placed in your heart? What do you long to see most in the Kingdom? Healing? Reconciliation? Freedom for the oppressed? Comfort for the broken hearted? Helping those in need? Creating a safe and joyful space for people to gather? Reaching people who have never had the chance to hear about Jesus? The possibilities are endless, and God has placed something in you that no one else has. Let Him speak to you about that. Let Him call that up in you. Let Him share His heart with you and ignite that passion in you. Then let Him show you the next step to take towards proclaiming and demonstrating His Kingdom in the way He created you to. This conversation, like all wonderful conversations with God, never truly ends. Write down what He shares with you and your experiences with Him.

_____

_____

_____

_____

_____

_____

BECOMING DEEPLY ROOTED

You may be asking yourself. Okay, now what? This book was designed to be not only a Bible study, but also a tool box that can be referred to over and over again as you continue to grow in your relationship with God. You may have found yourself asking God certain questions as you went through this book.

Keep practicing by asking Him good questions like: *What does this mean?* or *How do you want me to respond?* Keep listening for His voice and His leading.

This may be the end of the book, but it is the beginning of a new, exciting, life-giving adventure with God for you. As you close the pages of this book, my desire is that you will grab onto a new way of encountering God, and that you would continue to see His face more clearly, becoming more sensitive to His whispers, and increasingly confident that His promises are sure. My hope is that you will find yourself continually aware of His presence with you, that you will grow in your understanding of who God made you to be, and that you will be increasingly awed at His life at work in you as you become a bold proclaimer and miraculous demonstrator of the Kingdom!

 **PRAYER**

God, You are so good and faithful! You love walking with me and it has been my joy getting to know You better. Grab onto my hand, Lord, and take me even deeper into relationship with You. Show me the next step you would like to take with me, and empower me by Your Spirit to take that step. Continue to open my eyes that I may know You more, and make me more like You so that I can make You known to those around me.

Amen.

To contact Stacey Beebe or
to learn more about available products, visit:
Thegraftingproject.com

APPENDIX #ONE

THE NAMES AND CHARACTERISTICS OF GOD

Read this list out loud to God, saying "God, You are..."

- The Great I AM (Genesis 17:5))
- The God who sanctifies (1 Corinthians 6:11)
- Infinite (Romans 11:33)
- All-Powerful (Jeremiah 32:17)
- Good (1 Chronicles 16:34)
- Love (1 John 4:8)
- The God who provides (Matthew 6:26)
- The God of peace (Philippians 4:6-7))
- Ever perfect and unchanging (James 1:17)
- Just: We can trust You to always do what is right. (Psalm 75:2-3)
- Holy (Revelation 4:8-11)
- The God who heals (Psalm 103:2-3)
- Omniscient: All knowing (Psalm 139:4)
- Omnipresent: You are everywhere. (Psalm 139:7-12)

- Merciful: Your compassion never fails. (Lamentations 3:22)
- Sovereign: You are in control of our lives. (Job 42:2)
- Wise (Job 12:13)
- Faithful (1 Corinthians 1:4-9)
- Full of Grace (Hebrews 4:16)
- Our Comforter (2 Corinthians 1-3)
- God Almighty (1 Chronicles 29:11)
- Father (Romans 8:15-17)
- Head of the Church (Ephesians 1:22-23)
- Intercessor (Hebrews 4:14-16)
- Patient (Psalm 86:15)
- Kind (Ephesians 2:7)
- Counselor (Isaiah 9:6)

APPENDIX #TWO

THE PROMISES OF GOD

Declare this list out loud to yourself. It's very powerful when you put your name in it as you declare each scripture over yourself.

- Exodus 14:4 "The LORD will fight for you; you need only to be still."
- Deuteronomy 31:8 "The LORD Himself goes before you and will be with you; He will never leave you nor forsake you. Do not be afraid; do not be discouraged."
- Joshua 1:5 "I will never leave you nor forsake you."
- Psalm 34:17 "The righteous cry out, and the LORD hears them; He delivers them from all their troubles."
- Psalm 34:18 "The LORD is near to the brokenhearted and saves those who are crushed in spirit."
- Psalm 145:9 "The LORD is good to all; He has compassion on all He has made."
- Isaiah 40:29 "He gives strength to the weary and increases the power of the weak."

- Isaiah 40:31 "But those who hope in the LORD will renew their strength. They will soar on wings like eagles; they will run and not grow weary, they will walk and not be faint."
- Isaiah 41:10 "So do not fear, for I am with you; do not be dismayed, for I am your God. I will strengthen you and help you; I will uphold you with my righteous right hand."
- Isaiah 43:2 "When you pass through the waters, I will be with you; and when you pass through the rivers, they will not sweep over you. When you walk through the fire, you will not be burned; the flames will not set you ablaze."
- Isaiah 53:5 "But He was pierced for our transgressions, He was crushed for our iniquities; the punishment that brought us peace was on Him, and by His wounds we are healed."
- Isaiah 54:10 "'Though the mountains be shaken and the hills be removed, yet my unfailing love for you will not be shaken nor my covenant of peace be removed,' says the LORD, who has compassion on you."
- Isaiah 54:17 "'No weapon forged against you will prevail, and you will refute every tongue that accuses you. This is the heritage of the servants of the LORD, and this is their vindication from me,' declares the LORD."
- Isaiah 66:13 "As a mother comforts her child, so I will comfort you."
- Jeremiah 17:14 "Heal me, O LORD, and I shall be healed; save me, and I shall be saved; for you are my praise."
- Jeremiah 29:11 "For I know the plans I have for you, declares the LORD, plans to prosper you and not to harm you, plans to give you hope and a future."
- Jeremiah 29:12 "Then you will call on me and come and pray to me, and I will listen to you."

- Nahum 1:7 "The LORD is good, a refuge in times of trouble. He cares for those who trust in Him."
- Matthew 6:31-33 "So do not worry, saying, 'What shall we eat?' or 'What shall we drink?' or 'What shall we wear?' For the pagans run after all these things, and your Heavenly Father knows that you need them. But seek first His kingdom and His righteousness, and all these things will be given to you as well."
- Matthew 7:7 "Ask and it will be given to you; seek and you will find; knock and the door will be opened to you. For everyone who asks receives; the one who seeks finds; and to the one who knocks, the door will be opened."
- Matthew 11:28-30 "Come to me, all you who are weary and burdened, and I will give you rest. Take my yoke upon you and learn from me, for I am gentle and humble in heart, and you will find rest for your souls. For my yoke is easy and my burden is light."
- Mark 11:24 "Therefore I tell you, whatever you ask for in prayer, believe that you have received it, and it will be yours."
- John 8:36 "So if the Son sets you free, you are free indeed."
- John 14:27 "Peace I leave with you; my peace I give you. I do not give to you as the world gives. Do not let your hearts be troubled and do not be afraid."
- Romans 8:32 "He who did not spare His own Son, but gave Him up for us all – how will He not also, along with Him, graciously give us all things?"
- Philippians 4:6-7 "Do not be anxious about anything, but in every situation, by prayer and petition, with thanksgiving, present your requests to God. And the peace of God, which transcends all understanding, will guard your hearts and your minds in Christ Jesus."

- Philippians 4:19 "And my God will meet all your needs according to the riches of His glory in Christ Jesus."
- Romans 8:28 "And we know that in all things God works for the good of those who love Him, who have been called according to His purpose."
- Romans 8:38-39 "For I am sure that neither death nor life, nor angels nor rulers, nor things present nor things to come, nor powers, nor height nor depth, nor anything else in all creation, will be able to separate us from the love of God in Christ Jesus our LORD."

APPENDIX #THREE

WHO I AM IN CHRIST

(ORIGINALLY COMPILED BY NEIL ANDERSON)

Declare this list out loud to yourself.

John 1:12	I am God's child.
John 15:15	I am a friend of Jesus Christ.
Romans 5:1	I have been declared righteous
1 Corinthians 6:17	I am united with the LORD, and I am one with Him in spirit.
1 Corinthians 6:19-20	I have been bought with a price, and I belong to God.
1 Corinthians 12:27	I am a member of Christ's body.
Ephesians 1:3-8	I have been chosen by God and adopted as His child.
Colossians 1:13-14	I have been redeemed and forgiven of all my sins.
Colossians 2:9-10	I am complete in Christ.

Hebrews 4:14-16	I have direct access to the throne of grace through Jesus Christ.
Romans 8:1	I am free from condemnation.
Romans 8:28	I am assured that God works for my good in all circumstances.
Romans 8:38-39	I cannot be separated from the love of God.
2 Corinthians 1:21-22	I have been established, anointed, and sealed by God.
Colossians 3:1-4	I am hidden with Christ in God.
Philippians 1:6	I am confident that God will complete the good work He started in me.
Philippians 3:20	I am a citizen of Heaven.
2 Timothy 1:7	I have not been given a spirit of fear, but of power, love, and a sound mind.
1 John 5:18	I am born of God, and the evil one cannot touch me.
John 15:5	I am a branch of Jesus Christ, the true vine, and a channel of His life.
John 15:16	I have been chosen and appointed to bear fruit.
1 Corinthians 3:16	I am God's temple.
2 Corinthians 5:17-21	I am a minister of reconciliation for God.
Ephesians 2:6	I am seated with Jesus Christ in the heavenly realm.
Ephesians 2:10	I am God's workmanship.
Ephesians 3:12	I can approach God with freedom and confidence.
Philippians 4:13	I can do all things through Christ, who strengthens me.

Made in the USA
Monee, IL
15 April 2021